CW00507994

Cover Design: Mina Rose

Principles of Collaboration

ISBN: 978-1-0686660-1-8

Acknowledgements

Thank you to:

Les Druitt for his support, guidance, kindness and intellectual stimulation. And, for demonstrating that it's possible to be a strong business professional and a genuinely warm and caring person at the same time.

John Pirtle for directly and positively contributing to the concepts outlined in this book and for many years of coaching, encouragement and, most of all, friendship.

Richard Harris for reviewing the account of the incredible Tham Luang Nang Non Cave rescue in which he played an instrumental role.

Mike O'Keefe for fact checking the writing on Ross Perot and the early days of Electronic Data Systems.

Tracy Edwards for reviewing the précis of the inspiring story of *Maiden* in the 1989/90 Whitbread Round the World Race —and for her inspiring words of encouragement and support.

Michael Conlin and Amy Claire Wild for taking the time to review early copies of the manuscript and provide invaluable recommendations for adjustments and improvements.

Amelia Rose Alderson, for the cover design.

And lastly, but MOST IMPORTANTLY, Alison Alderson for her countless hours of reviewing, editing and advising on multiple versions of the manuscript—and for being an extraordinary partner, mother and soulmate.

ii

Preface
(by Roger Alderson)

I always thought that it would be easy to write a business book. Then I sat down and tried for myself.

I discovered that it isn't at all easy: quite the contrary, it's very difficult. Even when equipped with ideas and processes that are already documented and have been honed over many years in a wide variety of situations, it's still astonishingly difficult to assemble that content into a book—especially a book that somebody will take the time to read. It doesn't matter how much you write, re-write, and then re-write some more—it just never seems to be complete.

For this book, I first started jotting down ideas more than a decade ago, when I was a divisional marketing director for a large US-based technology company. I'd been in the role for a few years, joining when my original company was acquired in a massive, multi-billion dollar, corporate takeover.

At first I was excited to be part of this new corporate entity, but it soon became painfully obvious that, although the acquiring company had a rich history of innovative thinking and active collaboration, it was now an awkward behemoth of divisions, business units and geographies that operated largely independently within a cumbersome corporate environment.

It displayed a good face to the market—with an extensive suite
of consistently branded products and services—but beneath
the surface it was lacking a cohesive market strategy and the
corporate offerings were poorly integrated. Executive
leadership was weak, interdivisional alignment was limited,
internal competition was extensive, and corporate
collaboration was evident in only a few pockets of excellence.

But, it was the success of these few pockets of
collaborative excellence that prompted me to begin paying
closer attention.

The internal groups that worked together to solve
problems or realise opportunities were clearly more successful
than those that didn't. The people working in these groups
were more highly engaged, more enthusiastic and more
fulfilled than those elsewhere in the company. Perhaps most
important of all, the products and services created by these
groups were more innovative, more closely aligned to market
needs, and of notably higher quality than those created in
other parts of the organisation.

Of course, this wasn't particularly shocking and
chances are this isn't a surprise to anybody reading this book;
most people are very aware of the the value of effective
teamwork. In every organisation around the world there are
quotes posted on notice boards saying things like "*If everyone
moves forward together, success takes care of itself*", or "*Teamwork makes
common people achieve uncommon results*", or "*Talent wins games but
teamwork and intelligence win championships*".

But, although it's easy to make expansive statements
about teamwork, actually pulling it off isn't quite so simple.
To simply assemble a group of people and tell them to '*get on
with it*' is rarely a recipe for success. It takes talent, vision and
effort to establish a truly collaborative environment—*and even
more talent, vision and effort to maintain it.*

So, I started to review my past experiences of what
had worked and what hadn't when collaborating with others,
and combined them with observations of the pockets of
expertise in my new environment—actively looking for the
common factors that spawned success.

The notes that I made turned out to be incredibly
useful. I have since used them many times, applying them to
both small-team initiatives and massive multi-organisational
ventures—adjusting and refining them based on variations in
circumstances. As an independent consultant, they have been

invaluable tools for me in strategy engagements and especially valuable when helping to facilitate cooperative business ventures.

The stimulus to finally assemble my notes into a book came in 2019 during conversations with Les Druitt and John Pirtle of Integris Applied, a small but highly respected technology services intermediary firm that was an important client for me. We were talking about the challenges of an IT business model known as multi-sourcing, where several technology vendors come together to provide an integrated service to a client; Les and John were lamenting that very few such agreements were truly collaborative. Instead, they suggested that the vast majority of multi-sourcing agreements consisted of a federation of suppliers, each of which focused on providing their individual deliverables but didn't feel any real obligation to move beyond that. In those environments, if one specific supplier failed to deliver effectively, well, that was their problem.

But, they noted that when multi-sourcing environments were truly collaborative, and suppliers genuinely worked together to deliver a unified solution, the results were spectacular—orders of magnitude better than when they operated independently.

As we talked, I realised that the characteristics of collaborative multi-sourcing IT environments were essentially the same as those of *any* collaborative environment. In fact, I realised that no matter the industry, the objective, the size, or the nature of collaboration, there are some basic universal approaches that are consistent and reliable drivers of success for when people work together. It was this realisation that prompted me to finally sit down and start writing.

But, it has taken quite a while to get to something that resembles a book. Other commitments have got in the way and, contrary to how I imagined it would go, the words haven't just poured out of me and onto the page. Rather, they've splashed, splattered and sploshed. It's taken a lot of effort, and an inordinate amount of time, to massage them into something that is at least somewhat readable.

The book took a leap forward when my daughter, Isabelle, started working on it with me. As a recent psychology graduate, she had some interesting and useful perspectives on how and why people work together. As we chatted, I realised that she had a lot to offer in terms of content; her insights and opinions have been instrumental in shaping the final structure of the book, and pushing me to create something above and beyond a list of dos and don'ts.

I hope that you find what Isabelle and I have created to be interesting, informative or—at the very least—thought-provoking. If you do, buy another copy and give it to somebody as a gift. If you don't, educate us as to what you would do differently; we're always ready to learn about new ideas and approaches. In fact, we'd love to.

Of course, if you think that everything we've written is just common sense, and you could do better yourself, go ahead and give it a try. I assure you, it's much more difficult than it looks.

Preface
(by Isabelle Alderson)

Growing up with a love for nature, I spent much of my childhood observing the complex connections that support our natural world. I'd sit for hours watching streams of ants functioning as one in the pursuit of food or shelter: hundreds of small animals displaying a phenomenon that I now know is emergence. I'd watch how a fallen tree could transform into a home for beetles, spiders and earthworms, and help communities of fungi flourish.

As I got older and became more socially aware, I found myself observing human behaviour in a similar way— questioning such things as, why do some groups embrace collective success, while others don't?

Studying Sociology in school fed my curiosity, giving me possible explanations for my many questions. I fell in love with the subject, finding myself enthralled by the various case studies, intrigued or even provoked by existing theories, and increasingly impressed by the complexity of human connection. I had a particularly impactful teacher, Mrs Jenny Harrison, who brought passion and positivity to even the most difficult topics; she shaped my academic endeavours by encouraging me to challenge existing theories and to always consider the role of intersectionality before making assumptions. In doing so, I understood how impactful individual factors are in shaping any collective interaction, and this inspired me to undertake a degree in Psychology to explore these factors in greater depth.

Throughout my degree, even while studying the nuanced differences in individual cognition, the gregarious and social nature of mankind continued to underpin each module. Developmental Psychology emphasised the role of others in shaping a child's development, Business Psychology looked at individual contributions to a greater goal, Biological Psychology mapped out the neurological processes responsible for attraction, and Classification Systems defined 'abnormality' in reference to the wider population; even practical experiments required us to consider the many social factors that could influence or discredit a study outcome. I had more evidence than ever before that we humans, just like ants, are each a part of a larger whole. And, now a young adult entering the working world, I began to consider how this could be applied to an occupational setting.

Timing was in my favour: I happened to finish my degree just as my Dad was pulling together ideas for what would eventually become this book. We spoke about it together one evening and after I had made a few comments and observations from a psychological perspective, we discovered that I had some interesting contributions regarding the psychological processes that underpin collaboration. And so, we worked on it together.

Interestingly, the very task of collaborating on this book led me to re-visit and delve a lot deeper into much of what I've learned, so far—reaffirming my interest in connection, collaboration and motivation. It also allowed us to practice some of our own recommendations, and who doesn't love some applied learning?

Contents

Introduction

The human body is an incredibly complex collection of around thirty trillion cells. To put that hard-to-comprehend number into some kind of context, there are seventy-five times more cells in the average human than there are stars in the Milky Way. Yet, what's truly remarkable is that only about ten percent of these cells are actually ... human. The remaining ninety percent contain no human DNA at all. Instead, they are biological entities that coexist with us to combat disease, assist digestion, and transport essential materials throughout our bodies.

As an organism, we humans are the very model of active collaboration.

And, just as collaboration is essential to creating and sustaining the thing that is us, it is similarly important in accomplishing the things that we want to achieve. It allows us to do things better, cheaper and faster. Sometimes, it allows us to do things that would, otherwise, not be at all possible. Whether overcoming a problem, realising an opportunity, or just sharing an experience, we're better together.

Collaborating with others means accessing a broader range of skills and resources, with individual participants bringing new and different capabilities in the form of tools, processes, techniques, technologies, experiences, connections and expertise.

Collaborating with others means applying more collective neurones to a problem or opportunity, which in turn translates into more perspectives, ideas and opinions.

> *"I not only use all the brains that I have, but also all that I can borrow."*
> **Woodrow Wilson**

Collaborating with others increases focus and commitment while simultaneously fostering esprit de corps, where the rewards of success—and consequences of failure—extend far beyond individual achievements, encouraging everyone to push a little harder and aspire to higher standards.

Collaborating with others saves or even creates time—the most precious and least renewable commodity in the universe. When there are more people focused on a target outcome, there is more collective time available to achieve it.

And finally, *collaborating with others* enriches day-to-day activities because shared experiences are stronger, deeper and more meaningful than individual experiences. Sometimes, the single most important reason for working with other people—occasionally the only reason for working with other people—is quite simply because it's more enjoyable to do so.

Of course, not all collaborative efforts are the same and the concept of collaboration exists on a spectrum.

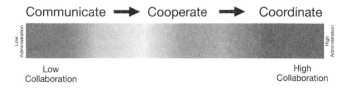

At its most basic it is simply good **communication**—people talking to one another to share ideas and information. It requires little in the way of structure or organisation and is really just a matter of tapping into, and participating in, relevant, timely and productive conversations. It's a simple but effective form of collaboration and is the reason that there are so many forums, discussion groups, clubs and societies. The ability to tap into the insight, experience and ideas of others provides tangible benefits such as alternative viewpoints, sounding boards for new concepts, and exposure to the latest tools and techniques.

At a slightly higher level, collaboration is **coordination**—people making a conscious effort to align their activities around a shared goal that can be achieved more easily or effectively as a group. At this level, participants actively embrace the value of working together and willingly sacrifice some amount of individual success for group success, understanding that the increased potential for benefit comes at a price. They also recognise that as the scope, scale and complexity of collaboration increases, so too does the need for administration, and well-coordinated collaboration requires process and structure to achieve its goals.

At its most advanced, collaboration is about **cooperation**—people directly contributing effort and expertise to a group effort because a common goal is difficult, or perhaps even impossible, to achieve alone. At this level, each person brings something tangible that contributes to overall success, and without which the target outcome would be orders of magnitude more difficult. The trade-off is increased operational complexity and the need for professional-grade orchestration and administration to maintain group focus and commitment. Just bringing people together isn't enough; even people with common interests and an obvious need to work together won't do so unless somebody takes the initiative and makes it happen.

Humans may be naturally social creatures, with an inbuilt affinity for interaction, but collaboration must still be initiated, cultivated and nurtured.

And that's what this book is all about—the initiation, cultivation and nurturing of collaborative endeavours. No matter if the collaboration is structured around a small project requiring a handful of individuals or a massive global initiative with a cast of thousands, this book contains practical approaches for helping people and organisations be …

… better together.

Formulate

Dreams only ever come true if they are clear in the mind of the dreamer

In any group endeavour there is always a broad array of ideas and opinions. It's natural for people from different backgrounds and experiences to have different perspectives, and even people from similar backgrounds can experience the same situation and make different interpretations of it— sometimes substantially different interpretations.

Most of the time this is a good thing. In fact, it's often a great thing, and is one of the reasons that working in diverse teams is so interesting and rewarding. Rather than being siloed and stagnant, diverse-team thinking is expansive and free flowing. Not only do participants bring a wide range of perspectives and ideas, they also bring different reasons for participating and different ways of doing so. It's a bit of a cliché, but diverse teams are genuinely 'a rich melting pot' of opinions and approaches that are a core foundation of success.

But, one aspect of group effort where a diversity of opinion is *not* advantageous is the collective understanding of a target outcome. Each participant in an endeavour may have their own style, perspective, approach and reasons for getting involved, but success is heavily dependent on all participants having a common understanding and appreciation of what everybody is striving to achieve.

That common understanding can be established by developing a carefully crafted *statement of purpose* that clearly and unambiguously outlines the target outcome: providing everybody with a straightforward understanding of *what* should be achieved, *why*, and by *when*. It won't completely eliminate divergent views across the endeavour, but it will make them less likely—helping people align their thinking and have the same core objective in mind.

> **Components of a**
> **Statement of Purpose**
>
> Vision
> Motivation
> Timeframe

There are three key components to a statement of purpose, of which **vision** is the first—a brief narrative that describes the target outcome in the most simple and succinct manner possible. It should be long enough to fully define it while being short enough to be understandable and memorable. Of course, as anybody who has tried to craft a short, pithy statement knows, this isn't easy—especially in a group setting where there is a broad range of interests and opinions. A long and verbose statement is much easier to create than a short and succinct one[1] because it encompasses more perspectives and includes multiple points of view, which in turn avoids hurt feelings and minimises conflict and disagreement. But, despite its benefits, a verbose statement also reduces clarity and opens the door to divergent or conflicting interpretations—a potentially fatal shortcoming for a collaborative endeavour.

A good approach is to start by creating an initial vision without worrying too much about length. Multiple opinions can be represented, a variety of perspectives catered to, and people contributing will feel that their voices are heard. Then, prune out those aspects that aren't absolutely necessary until only the core essence remains. It may mean that the more tangential and esoteric elements of the vision are omitted from the final version but, since the aim is to create something that everybody can understand and align to—rather than something that covers every possible angle of interpretation—this is acceptable. During the process of reduction, people should maintain a feeling that they contributed but appreciate that not every perspective can be included in the final narrative.

If in doubt, a good test is to try and make the vision short enough that it can be recited in no more than two to three breaths. It isn't a hard and fast rule, and there are times when more words are required, but once the vision gets to the point that it needs *more* than three breaths to recite, it's almost certainly too long.

The second component of a statement of purpose is **motivation**, which extends the purpose beyond simply achieving something, to achieving it for a reason—an important additional facet that elevates the sense of engagement that people will feel for it. Achieving something for a reason is a complex topic and the subject of extensive intellectual and practical debate, but in general, humans are typically motivated by three basic needs:

- **Physical Motivation:** is based on a desire for increased health, safety or security.
- **Social Motivation:** is based on finding a sense of belonging, inclusion or connectivity.
- **Epicureal Motivation:** is based on the simple pursuit of fulfilment, enjoyment or pleasure.

Key Human Motivations

PRIMARY

Physical – health, safety, strength and security

Social – belonging, inclusion and connectivity

Epicureal – happiness, enjoyment and pleasure

SECONDARY

Commercial – money, assets and possessions

Political – influence, power and leverage

Informational – knowledge, understanding and ability

While these basic needs underlie most human actions, collaborative endeavours are more typically driven by secondary motivations. *Commercial* motivation is the most obvious, and is based on the expectation of a highly tangible reward such as money, property or assets. The second most common is *political* motivation, based on an expectation of an influence-oriented reward such as authority, power or leverage. Finally, the third most common motivation is *informational*, driven by a knowledge-based reward such as understanding, experience or insight.

Clarifying motivation within a statement of purpose might seem like an unnecessary and purely academic task, but it has genuine value. Taking the time to think about why people would want to collaborate on achieving a vision is an important step towards ensuring that they will continue to want to work on it, and will remain engaged throughout the lifetime of an endeavour. It also provides the basis for communicating the importance of an endeavour to a wider audience and persuading people to support it. Different people will have different interests, but taking the time to understand what the core motivations could be will help attract people to the endeavour and possibly encourage them to participate.

The third and final component of the statement of purpose is a **timeframe**. On the surface this may appear to be the easiest element of all—since all that's required is to set a date by which the endeavour will achieve its target outcome. But, like a lot of seemingly simple things, this can be much more nuanced than it might first appear. Defining a timeframe is actually a delicate balance between credibility and urgency—credibility so that people can clearly imagine the vision being achieved within the stated timeframe, and urgency so that they see it happening quickly enough for them to tangibly benefit from it.

A timeframe that is too aggressive will result in the loss of participant confidence. This can happen immediately when people look at the completion date, make an assessment that it simply isn't possible, and mentally disengage from it. Other times it will happen later, as milestones are missed, trust is eroded and morale inevitably drops. At the other end of the spectrum, a timeframe that is too relaxed results in the endeavour taking longer than necessary or, in the worst-case scenario, not being achieved at all because participants deprioritise effort due to a misguided attitude that '*there'll be time to get to that later*'.

During the very early stages of an endeavour, it's acceptable for a timeframe to be adjusted and tweaked during discussion and debate. But, once the endeavour is fully underway, the timeframe needs to remain constant. Participants need to feel fully confident that it is a fixed point in time and every conceivable effort will be made to meet it.

The reality is, an inability to establish good timeframes is a problem, and a failure to operate within them is an even bigger problem. So, although it might seem like timeframe is the simplest element of the statement of purpose, in reality it's probably the most difficult and requires finding the often elusive sweet spot between ambition and practicality.

CASE STUDY
Komatsu vs Caterpillar

An excellent case study of the power of a good statement of purpose, and the impact that it can have on commercial success, is the story of Japan-based Komatsu K.K. vs US-based Caterpillar Inc.

The companies had been fierce rivals in the heavy industrial equipment market for decades, a rivalry that came to a head in the mid-1960s when Caterpillar formed a strategic alliance with Mitsubishi to directly challenge Komatsu in its home market. This prompted Komatsu to define a new strategic intent specifically targeted at its competitor—*"Encircle Caterpillar"* ("丸丁字"), a concept based on the strategically complex Chinese board game 'Go' where the core objective is to surround an opponent's pieces with your own and thereby claim territory.

As a statement, although *Encircle Caterpillar* has power and strength, it is distinctly lacking in specificity and timeframe. And yet, it is credited with being instrumental to Komatsu's global success and is included in the syllabi of business schools around the world. So, why was it so successful?

It's because *Encircle Caterpillar* wasn't actually Komatsu's statement of purpose. Rather, it was a slogan specifically developed to focus the attention of the workforce, at every level, during an expansion into the US market. An expansion that was both a defensive reaction to Caterpillar's expansion plans and a counter-attack to push harder into global markets.

Komatsu's full statement of purpose at the time was much more expansive:

Establish long-term growth and strong financial performance by attaining global dominance of the heavy industrial equipment through:
1) *the adoption of all relevant leading technologies from around the globe,*
2) *the improvement of quality standards throughout the organisation, and*
3) *the expansion and enhancement of a global dealer network.*

Although it's missing a timeframe, it does have the other primary components of a strong statement of purpose: vision (global dominance) and motivation (growth and financial performance). It even defines three key competitive battlegrounds—technology, quality and a dealer network—all of which were seen as essential to long-term success. It's a simple but clear statement that defines exactly what the ambition of the organisation was and the priorities to focus on.

The true brilliance of Komatsu's approach was to combine an already succinct statement of purpose with a beautifully crisp and engaging slogan, in the process setting in motion an internal culture of exceptional drive and ambition. It spawned a sequence of corporate initiatives that exploited weaknesses in Caterpillar and established a growing strategic advantage. Komatsu relentlessly improved quality, drove down costs, cultivated export markets and invested in new product development—all basic business improvements that would probably have led to success anyway, but within an inspired framework that galvanised focus across the entire organisation and fuelled a culture of excellence.

The Komatsu story illustrates how a strong statement of purpose can be a fundamental tool for helping people work together towards a common objective. It exemplifies how everybody can have the same perception of a target outcome, even when some participants have secondary, tertiary or even tangential aspirations. And, when fused with an engaging slogan, it shows how a statement of purpose can go far beyond getting participants to merely think alike; it can also act as a powerful rallying cry that brings people together to achieve something collectively worthwhile.

However, even the most powerful rallying cry will lose impact without some understanding of what must be achieved to realise it, and that's the next step in formulating a strategic endeavour—developing goals.

Establishing goals is one of the oldest and most widely acknowledged contributors to success. Their importance has been recognised for millennia. Seneca, a Roman philosopher and advisor to Nero, said "*If one doesn't know which port one is sailing to, no wind is favourable*". Solon, an Athenian statesman, said "*In all things you do, consider the end*". More recently, Cecil Mace (in the 1930s), Edwin Locke (in the 1960s), Franklin Covey (in the 1980s) and Douglas Vermeeren (in the 1990s) all built professional reputations and lucrative careers on advocating the importance of goal setting as a foundational element to personal and business success.

> "One day Alice came to a fork in the road and saw a Cheshire cat in a tree. 'Which road do I take?' she asked. 'Where do you want to go?' was his response. 'I don't know,' Alice answered. 'Then,' said the cat, 'it doesn't matter."
> **Alice in Wonderland**
> *Lewis Carroll*

Goals are especially important in collaborative endeavours where there are multiple personalities striving to achieve something together. They:

- **Focus Attention:** on the most important aspects of the endeavour and—perhaps more importantly—away from those that are less important. Time is the most valuable and least renewable commodity in the universe and 'focus' ensures it is consumed selectively.
- **Cultivate Perseverance:** to maintain effort even when the path to success is paved with obstacles and setbacks, which it frequently is. When goals are clearly defined, collaborators are more likely to find ways to work around issues and deal with problems.
- **Provide a Framework for Flexibility**: where action can be refined and adjusted as situational dynamics change. Setting goals makes it easier to understand progress and recognise when, and what, adjustments are needed to achieve the purpose. After all, it's difficult to move to plan B if there was never a plan A.

The fact is, goals are much more than just sub-targets: they establish a sense of direction and in the process guide decision making. For groups, they stimulate a culture of ambition and achievement and nurture team spirit where the sum is truly greater than the parts.

Well-defined goals have four key attributes, the first of which is **specificity**. They are articulated as clearly and concisely as possible in terms of *what* must be achieved, by *how much*, and *when*.[2] Just like a statement of purpose, the more specific a goal, the easier it is to visualise and the greater the chances are of achieving it. When an end result is clear, the paths available to achieving it are correspondingly easier to see, and this is especially true in highly diverse environments with people from different backgrounds and experiences. High specificity increases the chances that everybody has the same fundamental understanding of key objectives and will work together to achieve them.

> **Attributes of a Goal**
>
> Specificity
> Relevance
> Attainability
> Attribution

Relevance is the second core attribute, and means ensuring that a goal is clearly aligned to the overall purpose of the endeavour. The greater the relevance, the greater the engagement of the collaborative community, and engaged collaborators have high enthusiasm and dedication towards not just individual goals, but to the endeavour generally. Engaged collaborators understand that their individual effort makes a collective difference. They care about their contribution *and* about the performance of those around them, so the more relevant the goal the stronger the engagement, and therefore the greater the chance of achieving it.

Attainability is the third attribute and is focused on how challenging a goal is. On the one hand, there is a strong argument for setting ambitious goals, even highly ambitious goals that stretch all participants to strive for the best possible outcome. One of history's greatest achievers, Michelangelo, said "*The greater danger for most of us isn't that our aim is too high and we miss, but that it's too low and we hit*". But, on the other hand, although a goal should possess stretch, it should also be grounded in reality. If a goal isn't credible, goal commitment —the extent to which a community is focused on reaching it—

drops dramatically. So, the trick is to set challenging but attainable goals, with acceptable fall-back options that may not be exactly what was intended but still represent an acceptable outcome that contributes to the target outcome.

The fourth and final attribute of a well-defined goal is **attribution**, the identification of the owner responsible for achieving it. A common opinion is that individual goals should be the responsibility of individual people—the logic being that having one person fully accountable means that they are highly motivated to achieve it. It also simplifies measurement and monitoring because there is only one data source for status. However, an expansion of this position is to assign *two* people to a goal. This introduces an added element of peer pressure where two goal owners both have responsibility to ensure that the goal is achieved. At the same time it doesn't significantly increase the difficulty of measurement and monitoring, and there is even an argument that it increases transparency; having two data sources lessens the chance that two people will both misreport or misrepresent progress.

It's important to note that collaborative goal setting is different from individual goal setting because of the added dimension of mutual benefit. Where individual goals are driven by a desire for individual achievement, collaborative goals are based on group achievement, an extension that taps into one of the more esoteric but powerful drivers of human behaviour—the desire to be part of something bigger. The logical extension of this is that collaborative goal setting should, whenever possible, be a group activity—perhaps only a small core group during the preliminary stages of an endeavour, but a group nonetheless.

There are lots of ways to do this, and what works with one group may not work in another, but a tried-and-tested process that is effective in the majority of instances involves three key steps.

First, everybody individually brainstorms all of the goals that should be accomplished to reach the target outcome. Second, the goals are assembled onto a board (physical or virtual) and rationalised (clarifying each goal), de-duplicated (removing those that are the same) and consolidated (grouping those that are subsets of one another). And third, they are clearly defined, describing each goal from the four perspectives of specificity, relevance, attainability and ownership.

It's worth noting that it's common for goals to be continually refined throughout these three steps. Some that may seem very different at the start of the process begin to blend together as they are more closely scrutinised, while others become more obviously different. Similarly, new goals can emerge as discussion around achieving one unearths the need for another.

There is a fourth optional step that can be worthwhile considering: to make a preliminary assessment of the difficulty of achieving each goal. If there is just a handful to consider it isn't really worth the effort, but if a lot of goals are identified then it's worth prioritising them in terms of difficulty so that it's clear which will require the most attention, the most resources, and the most careful monitoring.

This doesn't have to be a long and drawn-out exercise: simply ask the question "*How difficult will this goal be to achieve?*" and then grade each accordingly. A four-level grading system is usually a good idea, because it avoids a middle ground and forces some differentiation between slightly more and slightly less difficult.[3] For example:

- **Manageable:** this goal will be relatively easy to achieve and the path to achieving it is clear.
- **Demanding:** this goal will be more difficult to achieve although the path to achieving it is relatively straightforward.
- **Challenging:** this goal will be very difficult to achieve and aspects of the path to achieving it are not immediately obvious.
- **Formidable:** this goal will be exceptionally difficult to achieve and aspects of the path to achieving it are unknown.

In most instances, preliminary goal-setting sessions can be conducted in one full day—with breaks and occasional sidebar discussions built into the schedule. However, for more complex endeavours with larger teams, especially those that require virtual sessions with participants joining from different time zones, it can be necessary to spread the effort over several days. In these instances, the efficiency of the exercise will be significantly enhanced if group members are informed beforehand of what will be expected of them, and are given an idea of the general structure and flow that the session will take. They will then not only be more mentally prepared for what is to come, but will also have time to pre-think ideas that they would like to bring to the discussion.

No matter what approach is used, it's important to understand that goal setting for a collaborative endeavour is not a one-off exercise. Rather, it's an ongoing, iterative process. During the early stages, the group is typically small and there is a lack of perfect clarity. It's highly likely for there to be unanswered questions, so preliminary goals are just that, preliminary. As the endeavour matures, more information is gathered, more participants join, and experience[4] and expertise are drawn into it. Goals can then be adjusted and refined based on greater understanding. It's also not unknown for key dynamics surrounding the endeavour to change over time, forcing associated goal adjustments.

But, even in instances when the paths towards it change, the purpose of the endeavour should remain constant and all goals should be directly tied to it. Strong goals, coupled with a well-defined statement of purpose, don't just enhance the likelihood of success, they become inextricably linked with it. They don't just boost success rates, they drive a deep sense of shared ownership and understanding of each individual's role within a broader context.

The plain truth is, no collaborative endeavour will reach its target outcome without a solid understanding of what must be accomplished to achieve it.

The Apollo Program

There are lots of good examples of statements of purpose, but one of the very best—and most famous—is from United States President John F. Kennedy in a speech made to the US Congress in May 1961. Despite the fact that it's more than 60 years old, chances are you'll recognise it:

John F. Kennedy - Image courtesy: Florida Memory

"I believe that this nation should commit itself to achieving the goal, before this decade is out, of landing a man on the Moon and returning him safely to the Earth. No single [space] project in this period will be more impressive to mankind or more important for the long-range exploration of space. And none will be so difficult or expensive to accomplish."

It is an outstanding example of a powerful and deeply engaging statement of purpose.

The vision is clear and easily stated in one breath, *"landing a man on the Moon and returning him safely to the Earth"*. The timeframe is equally clear, *"within the decade"*, which at the time of the speech meant before 31 December 1969. And finally, the motivation is clear, *"no project will be more impressive to mankind"*, meaning that achieving the purpose would provide the United States with tremendous geopolitical global influence, power and leverage. Interestingly, Kennedy even included reference to the fact that this will be *"difficult"* and *"expensive"* to achieve because he knew that these aspects of the program would be seen as worthy challenges rather than insurmountable barriers. By focusing on the strength and ingenuity of the United States, Kennedy tapped into a deep and powerful motivation that captured the hearts and minds of the entire nation.

It's important to note that Kennedy's statement of purpose, like all great statements of purpose, was focused on the *outcome* rather than the *output*. It was prescriptive about the ends but not the means. He didn't spell out what would be required to put a man on the Moon, despite the fact that he had a reasonably good idea of what that was because he proposed a budget of $531 m for 1962 and a further $7-$9 bn every year until the end of the decade. Instead of getting into details that he was poorly qualified to present and that would inevitably change over time, he stuck to a succinct and engaging statement. He knew that the steps required to get a man to the Moon and back again could, and almost certainly would, change. But, the purpose itself would remain constant until either gloriously achieved or abandoned in disappointment and failure.

Unsurprisingly, the endeavour that Kennedy launched soon developed an extensive list of goals that required a cast of thousands. In many instances the goals represented aspirations that had never before been attempted, and encompassed a level of 'stretch' that pushed the very limits of human ingenuity. Over the course of the decade many of them were adjusted, although the core sentiment of them remained stable.

For example, the core goal of propulsion changed as different mission modes were explored. Some early-concept mission modes were based on the idea that a single unified vehicle would be launched from Earth, travel to (and land on) the Moon, then travel back. That would require a rocket capable of launching a 74,000 kg payload—something that, even today, would be astonishingly difficult. The final goal, while still incredibly ambitious, was more realistic:

Supply guided thrust to move a 45,000 kg payload from the Earth to the Moon and back again with (scheduled and as required) mid-course corrections throughout the mission.

The goal is very specific and although truly formidable, attainable. Understandably, the relevance of the goal isn't explicitly stated because it is obvious that unless achieved, it would be impossible to put a human on the Moon. In terms of responsibility, this fell to the team of NASA's chief rocket scientist and program leader, Werner Von Braun.

Another goal was associated with the communications system:

Provide tracking and communications capable of transmission ranges greater than 385,000 km, that unifies voice, television, telemetry, command, tracking and ranging into a single system of the lowest possible size, weight and complexity.

Here, the goal very specifically identifies that the communications system must operate at a range of the distance of the Moon from the Earth. This might seem obvious, but it was especially relevant because the first space communication systems only needed to operate at ranges of a few thousand kilometres—or even a few hundred—and could use UHF and VHF radio frequencies. The significantly increased distances associated with travel to the Moon meant that communications needed to move from radio into the microwave portion of the electromagnetic spectrum. Responsibility for the goal isn't explicitly stated, but the team leader for the 'Unified S-Band Communications System' was Harold Rosen, a senior engineer at the Hughes Aircraft Company.

One more key goal of the lunar program worth reviewing was associated with the development of the space suit (or 'Extravehicular Mobility Unit' in NASA-speak) that would allow humans to walk on the surface of the Moon. It was a marvel of engineering design that grew out of a goal to:

Develop an Extravehicular Mobility Unit that can be donned by a crew member with minimal/no support from other crew members, provide a self-contained and safe life-support environment with enough mobility to exit the Lunar Module spacecraft, conduct exploratory examinations of the lunar surface, and then return safely.

This goal is particularly interesting because it evolved from a preliminary form in 1961 to what was finally achieved in 1969. During some periods of the endeavour, the particulars of the goal changed on an almost weekly basis and ownership was often unclear. However, the core goal never lost validity and Joe Kosmo, senior project engineer at International Latex Corporation, was the person who ultimately led the team that designed and developed the iconic A7L space suit that Armstrong and Aldrin used during the Apollo 11 mission.

It's open to debate if placing a man on the Moon is mankind's greatest ever achievement, but there's no denying that it was an incredible accomplishment that still has the power to amaze. Apollo provides an awe-inspiring example of how to formulate a collaborative endeavour, and Kennedy's beautifully crafted statement of purpose not only clearly defined an audacious ambition, it galvanised the imagination of an entire nation. The NASA community (public and private enterprise collaborators) maintained a razor-sharp focus on that purpose—by establishing clearly defined goals, and associated action plans—that represented truly audacious ambitions.

Associate

*To work with others ...
you need others to work with*

Collaboration, by definition, involves multiple people working together to achieve something. So, the most fundamental requirement for any collaborative endeavour is a community of collaborators —a group of willing participants with appropriate capabilities who have an interest in joining forces to achieve something of collective value.

> *"The first method for estimating the intelligence of a ruler is to look at those they have around them."*
> **Il Principe**
> **Niccolo Machiavelli**

During the early stages, when an endeavour is forming, the number of participants can be very small. If the group possesses all of the required capabilities to achieve the target outcome, great. But if there are capability gaps, then the group needs to expand and new participants must be recruited to fill those gaps.

Some endeavours are 'gold rush' initiatives and people queue up to take part. This can be because the potential rewards for participation are enormous—like with the California Gold Rush. Other times, it's because a noteworthy individual or organisation is a key player and others want to get onboard with them. And, at yet other times it's because the purpose of the endeavour taps into a zeitgeist that resonates with prevailing attitudes and attracts a buzz of popularity and relevance.

But, these instances are rare.

Most of the time, effort must be invested in finding and recruiting participants to join a collaborative community, and often *a lot* of effort is required.

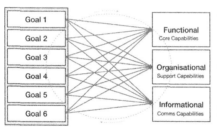

The process begins with understanding the capabilities—skills, assets and experiences—that a community needs to possess to achieve the target outcome. And this starts with a detailed examination of the goals of the endeavour, asking the question *"What functional, organisational and informational capabilities will be needed to achieve this goal?"*

Functional capabilities are those on which an endeavour is primarily based; they are the fundamental requirements without which it simply can't proceed. They are usually associated with core activities such as design, development and deployment.

Organisational capabilities are supporting elements that help an endeavour achieve and maintain operational viability. While not fundamentally essential to success, they are important catalysts or enablers. An endeavour might be able to achieve its target outcome without them, but it will operate much more smoothly with them. They typically include activities such as asset management, financial planning and human resources.

Finally, **informational capabilities** are those that ensure the smooth flow of information and ideas throughout a collaborative community, both internally and externally. They are communication vehicles and messages that inform, educate, inspire and influence, and include activities such as marketing, customer support and internal communications.

During the early stages of an endeavour, it isn't unusual for capabilities to be understood only at a superficial level. In fact, for particularly groundbreaking or innovative endeavours, it isn't unusual for some of them to be completely unknown at the outset. But, as an endeavour matures clarity increases and more capabilities are identified. That's when the focus shifts from just identifying a capability to more deeply understanding it and its importance.

A good way to do this, is to plot capabilities on a significance/urgency matrix—a visual representation of importance that can help focus attention on those capabilities that are most critical at any particular instance in time. The more important capabilities, and those that should be considered a priority, will appear in the top right of the matrix. The less immediately important capabilities, and those that can be assigned a lower priority, will be in the bottom left.[5]

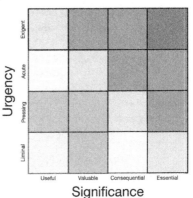

Significance, is how critical a capability is. Some will be essential and an endeavour will fail without them, whereas others will be merely useful, and an endeavour can still achieve its target outcome even if the capability is not fully brought to bear. A relatively simple technique is to grade each capability into one of four categories:

- **Useful**: a successful outcome will be possible without this capability but would be easier with it.
- **Valuable**: a successful outcome will be difficult, but not impossible, without this capability.

- **Consequential**: a successful outcome will be very challenging without this capability.
- **Essential**: a successful outcome will be impossible without this capability.

Urgency, is how quickly a capability must be integrated within the collaborative community. This is a more fluid consideration that can vary over time—ebbing and flowing as an endeavour progresses. Some capabilities will be needed immediately, whereas others will be required later. Once again, a four-level categorisation is a good grading mechanism:

- **Liminal**: Although not required immediately, the capability will be of value before the final stages of the endeavour.
- **Pressing**: the capability will become increasingly necessary as the endeavour progresses.
- **Acute**: the capability should be available as quickly as possible.
- **Exigent**: the capability must be fully available right at the start of the endeavour.

It's important to recognise that the fluid nature of significance and urgency means that the matrix is perpetually undefined and will evolve throughout the lifetime of an endeavour. This is why it's important to regularly revisit and re-assess to reduce the risk of an endeavour being stalled—or worse still completely derailed—by the sudden unexpected absence of an essential need. Each time the matrix is reviewed, capabilities should be re-plotted and an evaluation made of those that are now within the domain of the community and those that remain outstanding.

When searching for collaborators to bring particular capabilities, the first and most obvious place to look is with **immediate (pre-existing) networks**—friends, family and colleagues with whom strong relationships already exist. People within this group may not be the most highly qualified, highly motivated, or readily available; but they are the most easily accessible and a logical starting point for collaborator recruitment. Many endeavours are populated initially with the support of immediate networks—they're the obvious first port

of call to get an endeavour underway and establish early
momentum.

Some endeavours will be able to progress all the way
to the target outcome using only collaborators from immediate
networks, but most will require at least some broader expertise.
So, the next place to look is with **direct networks**—former
colleagues and acquaintances with whom basic relationships
have been established, albeit not deeply entrenched. Although
these contacts are less substantial than those in pre-existing
networks, they are known quantities who are likely to return
calls. A conversation should be possible and if nothing else
they can be a sounding board to gauge interest in the
endeavour, solicit feedback, or act as a conduit to other
potential collaborators.

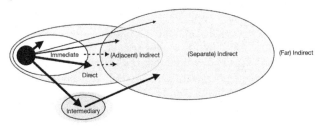

When a specific skill, asset or experience cannot be
found in immediate or direct networks, the third group to
explore is with **indirect networks**—people with whom no
prior relationship exists. Unfortunately, potential collaborators
in this group are very challenging to reach since they are
unknown quantities. The easiest way is by soliciting
recommendations from immediate or direct connections to
uncover *adjacent* indirect connections—a method that can yield
good results as recommendations for potential collaborators
can also be combined with introductions to them.

The least immediately accessible group is the *separate*
indirect networks, where no pre-existing relationships exist at
all. To access potential collaborators in this group it's
necessary to broadcast to places where potential collaborators
might see them. The easiest, and least expensive way of doing
this is via social media: making relevant posts across different
platforms to solicit interest. LinkedIn is particularly well-suited
due to its focus on professional networking, but more
consumer-oriented platforms (such as Facebook, Instagram
and X) can be useful too. Even content-biased platforms (such

as YouTube, Medium and Substack) can be used, although the success rate for these is likely to be low. Adopting an omni-channel approach, with messages integrated and coordinated across multiple platforms, creates the best results.

But, it's important to be realistic. Getting the right message in front of the right potential collaborator at the right time is exceptionally difficult. Response rates are low, and typically less that five percent of broadcast messages will reach the eyeballs of a potential collaborator—and less than two percent will elicit any kind of response. It's also important to understand that a drawback to this approach is that it often attracts attention from people who have an interest in the endeavour but lack the necessarily capabilities. This significantly increases the time and effort required to isolate those collaborators that have the greatest potential to contribute to the endeavour.

If there are still capability gaps after tapping into immediate, direct and indirect networks, there is one last method of finding collaborators that can be tried—using an **intermediary**. The concept isn't anything new and there have always been 'matchmakers' in commercial and personal environments—typically individuals or organisations with strong analytic skills supplemented by an extensive network of pre-existing connections. For example, in the professional world, accountants, lawyers, bankers and venture capitalists often facilitate mutually beneficial connections for their clients —sometimes for no cost but more often for either a direct fee or a portion of the eventual proceeds of an introduction.

There are also dedicated professional intermediaries for whom matchmaking is a full-time job. These people have expertise and extensive contacts within areas ranging from information technology to fine art. They are especially adept at finding rare, complex, expensive, or difficult-to-access capabilities, and although engaging their services can be expensive, it can also dramatically shortcut time and effort.

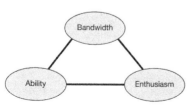

No matter from where a collaborator originates, it's crucial to assess their suitability, and that isn't just about selecting those with the strongest capabilities. Although demonstrable experience and expertise, or a valuable perspective, are obviously key attributes, they are only one of three core characteristics that should be considered. The second is the capacity and bandwidth to participate (since collaborators must have the time to get involved and bring their expertise to bear) and the third is a tangible interest in participation (because a strong collaborator should have something to gain from the outcome of the endeavour or, at the very least, the journey towards it).[6]

The reality is that highly qualified participants with great enthusiasm but lacking in bandwidth will not have the time to apply their expertise. Enthusiastic participants with lots of time but lacking in capability will not have the skills to contribute effectively. And, time-rich participants with the right capability but lacking in enthusiasm are the most risky of all because they may lose interest and disengage, potentially placing the entire endeavour at risk.

The challenge is to select collaborators who have the best balance of all three core attributes, plus other secondary attributes that further enhance their appeal. These secondary attributes will be unique to every endeavour, but there are eight that tend to be (reasonably) universal:

Collaborator Attributes
Bandwidth
Capability
Enthusiasm
Affinity
Perspective
Tolerance
Drive
Situational Awareness
Flexibility
Eloquence
Integrity

- **Affinity**: for the community and its purpose. Necessity may make for strange bedfellows,[7] and it isn't necessary for collaborators to be friends, but it is necessary for them to have a mutual respect for one another. If they demonstrate cultural, emotional and intellectual alignment to the endeavour and fellow participants, their value as a collaborator will be significantly enhanced.
- **Perspective**: that broadens the outlook of the entire community. It's always valuable when collaborators bring diversity of thinking to a collaborative endeavour, pushing boundaries and challenging pre-conceived notions.

Expansive thinking is what defines world-class endeavours, and collaborators who have a broad outlook will bring more ideas and opinions—something that often translates into a higher probability of achieving goals.

- **Tolerance**: for the ideas of others. Collaborators may have strong opinions and personal convictions, but they must be willing to listen to others and appreciate alternative points of view. The ability to recognise when to put aside small differences for the greater good is a strong asset, and even more important is a willingness to embrace unfamiliar viewpoints and make corresponding adjustments in personal perceptions.

- **Drive**: and a propensity for action. Collaborators should be doers more than dreamers, with an ability to establish, maintain or, even better, accelerate collective momentum. While creativity and vision are valuable traits, lots of people have good ideas and far fewer are capable of moving from idea to action.

- **Situational Awareness**: of potentially influential dynamics. Collaborators should be capable of assessing internal and external developments that could have a bearing on successfully achieving the purpose of an endeavour. It's important to be capable of reacting appropriately to different stimuli— including disregarding those that have low or no relevance.

- **Flexibility**: of action. Collaborators should be willing to embrace active learning, and adjust or refine their activity based on changing situations or personal limitations. Although the target outcome of an endeavour should remain constant, the path to achieving it can change as situations evolve and new information comes to light.

- **Eloquence**: of communication. Collaborators should be able to express themselves clearly and concisely, especially in complex situations where ambiguity or lack of clarity can create confusion. Miscommunication is very easy when people come from a variety of different backgrounds, so an ability to communicate clearly minimises unnecessary misunderstandings.

- **Integrity**: and an effective moral compass. Collaborators should have a demonstrable reputation for honesty, integrity and ethical behaviour. Although there are rare instances when the critical need for a specific capability may require the lowering of standards,[8] it is rarely—many would say never—a good idea to engage with an unreliable or untrustworthy collaborator.

Making the effort to assess every potential collaborator is inconvenient and time consuming, but absolutely necessary. It is all too common for potentially successful endeavours to founder because of a single poorly performing collaborator who wasn't assessed carefully enough. The old adage that one bad apple can spoil the barrel is very true. However, on the plus side, top-performing collaborators don't just bring their individual skills to the endeavour, they also act as catalysts for success and elevate performance across the board. Collaborators certainly don't need to possess all eight of the secondary attributes, but the more that they have, and the more strongly they can demonstrate them, the more aligned they are likely to be to the endeavour.[9]

The final step in sealing the relationship with a potential collaborator is to formalise it with a collaborator agreement. For more complex endeavours, this is an absolute necessity, but even for small-scale initiatives it's useful to clearly define roles and responsibilities, thereby avoiding misunderstandings later on. By focusing on the purpose of the relationship, and its expected evolution over time, all parties gain a clearer understanding of their role in achieving the target outcome of the endeavour. This clarity also provides an opportunity to identify and address concerns or obstacles sooner rather than later. After all, it's far preferable to fix, or even abandon, a potentially problematic relationship at the start, rather than later when disengagement could be far more detrimental.

For simple endeavours, the agreement can be as straightforward as defining roles and responsibilities along with some basic ground rules on topics such as confidentiality and finances. For more complex endeavours, it's better to take a more formal approach and agree on a series of key points. The most important areas to discuss and document are:

- **Obligations:** the role and responsibilities of each party, with an emphasis on what will be delivered, by when and with what level of resources and support.

- **Term and Termination:** the expected duration of the relationship and the conditions for ending it, including notification periods.

- **Confidentiality:** any restrictions to disclosure of information regarding the endeavour, intellectual property brought to it, or output from it.

- **Financial Factors:** details on funding, investment and revenue sharing aspects of the relationship.

- **Intellectual Property:** clarification of who owns what intellectual output(s), including any original concepts that emerge during the endeavour.

- **Project Management:** outlining of the project management approach to be utilised, including milestone management, metrics and controlling mechanisms.

- **Exclusivity:** restrictions on performing the same or similar work, or working with competitors, including time periods.

- **Non-Solicitation:** guidelines for pre-, post- and intra-endeavour relationship management with other parties to the endeavour.

- **Documents, Records and Data Protection:** how records and documents (including personal data) will be handled throughout the endeavour, and what level of security and transparency will be expected.

- **Dispute Resolution:** provisions for resolving disagreements, including mediation, arbitration or other resolution mechanisms.

- **Liability:** limitations on legal, financial and asset obligations.

CASE STUDY
The Apple II

A great example of the importance of finding the right people to associate with, is the development and launch of the Apple II personal computer, "*the greatest PC of all time*".[10]

The Apple II was actually the third commercial venture for high school friends Steve Wozniak and Steve Jobs. Their first was in 1971 when Wozniak developed a Little Blue Box, a digital device that allowed phone phreakers—early computer hackers—to manipulate the global telephone system. Jobs and Wozniak sold 200 of the (illegal) devices out of Wozniak's Berkeley dorm room for $150 each, making a tidy profit and signalling to Jobs that digital innovation could be fun AND highly profitable.

After that, Jobs and Wozniak's lives diverged for a while. Jobs enrolled in college, then dropped out, worked at Atari for a year, left to travel around India for eight months, returned to the US to live in an Oregon commune, and then finally returned to California to restart work at Atari. Wozniak took a marginally more traditional approach although he had a slight blip when he was expelled from the University of Colorado Boulder for hacking the university computer system. But, he then studied Electrical Engineering at Berkeley before starting a career at HP. They reconnected in 1974—after Jobs returned from Oregon—and from then on spent time together as friends and fellow technology enthusiasts.

The defining year of their lives was 1976, when Wozniak invented the Apple I, a motherboard-only computer that provided hobbyists with a gateway into the exciting new world of personal digital computers. He originally intended to give the design schematics away for free until Jobs persuaded him that there was a potential market to sell them. So, they reached out to Ronald Wayne—a respected administrator at Atari and colleague of Jobs—who helped them form a legal partnership. They then connected with Paul Terrell, a fellow member of the Menlo Park Homebrew Computer Club and owner of the retail outlet The Byte Shop[11] in Palo Alto, who agreed to sell 50 of the kits in his store. With an initial set of orders, they enlisted friends to help them assemble and distribute the kits, and ended up selling close to 200 units at $500 each (via retail channels) and $666 each (via direct sales) for a total revenue of $100,000 (equivalent to $500,000 in 2024).

Not bad for a couple of 20-somethings working out of a garage in Los Altos, California.

Even before sales of the Apple I had tailed off, Wozniak was working on the Apple II, a more advanced machine with the capability to connect peripheral devices such as printers, monitors and disk drives. As Wozniak finalised the design, Jobs realised that although they had established a strong circle of supporters, they needed broader capabilities if they were going to progress into a company that would be taken seriously in Silicon Valley.

His first step was to find somebody with capabilities in marketing and promotion. He had heard about a small firm that was building a strong reputation in the area, Regis McKenna Inc, so he picked up the phone and called its founder. Then he called again. And again. And several more times until, eventually, McKenna agreed to meet with him.

Unfortunately, that first meeting didn't go well.

Jobs and Wozniak brought a draft article written by Wozniak that they wanted to submit to Byte Magazine. McKenna thought that the article was interesting, but that it needed to be rewritten for a more consumer-oriented audience. Wozniak, an engineer through and through, disagreed and the meeting ended on a somewhat sour note.

But, later that day, Jobs called McKenna again and asked to meet with him again: alone this time. It was the start of an enduring relationship and they began meeting on a regular basis to discuss technology, business and marketing strategy. A by-product of the meetings was the development of the first Apple marketing plan in December 1976.[12]

From this point onwards, the collaborative community surrounding the Apple endeavour grew rapidly. McKenna introduced Mike Markkula—a former Fairchild Semiconductor and Intel executive—who invested $91,000 in the fledgling company, underwrote a $250,000 line of credit with Bank of America, and provided focused business advice. Markkula helped Jobs and Wozniak reposition Apple from a partnership into an incorporated company (on 3 January 1977) and brought in Michael Scott—a former colleague at Fairchild Semiconductor—as the company's first CEO. Other people with required skills and capabilities were also recruited: Bill Fernandez and Daniel Kottke provided additional engineering and production skills, Rod Holt developed the (unique at the time) Apple II power supply, Randy Wigginton focused on the BASIC programming language that came pre-installed with the system, Jerry Manock designed the case, Sherry Livingston provided day-to-day administration and Gary Martin handled accounting and finance.

By the time the Apple II was launched at the West Coast Computer Faire in April 1977, the company was a thriving community of complementary skills and capabilities, all working together to achieve something truly meaningful. It has been argued that the Apple II, along with the Commodore PET 2001 and the Tandy TRS-80 Model I, changed the world. That's debatable, but there's no argument that it was certainly massively successful. By the end of 1977, Apple had garnered revenues of $775,000 (equivalent to $4 m in 2024) and by the end of the decade—when it had added both a dedicated disk drive and the first ever 'killer app' in the form of VisiCalc—sales were $118 m ... and climbing.

Although the early days of Apple illustrate the importance of pulling together the right group of people, there is another important step to shaping those people into a community: providing a structured environment in which to work so that collaborators perform at their full potential.[13] This means a space (the arena), a language (the lexicon) and a set of rules (the guiding principles).

The **arena** is the place where collaborators assemble to talk, explore ideas, build understanding, resolve issues and draw conclusions. In the past this was a physical space such as an operations centre— sometimes called a 'war room'— where individuals, information and ideas came together. People would assemble in or near that space and work together to achieve a target outcome. Key participants were typically co-located, or at least near-located, and remote collaboration by phone, email or physical mail was used only when absolutely necessary or as an additional dimension to augment face-to-face interaction.

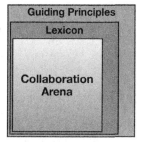

The concept of an operations centre for a collaborative endeavour is still popular today but is typically undertaken, at least in part, as a virtual space using digital collaboration tools. This increased flexibility means that collaborators can be physically dispersed, with geography and therefore time zone and travel budget playing a less critical role than in the past. While there's still no real substitute for face-to-face interaction, the powerful benefit of virtual spaces is that collaborators who would otherwise be unable to get involved can be included. People can be on entirely different continents and work together; the fundamental elements of the arena remain the same—a space where collaborators can interact—but the arena itself is typically a blend of physical and virtual.

When setting up a collaboration arena of any type, there are two key attributes that should be considered. The first is *temporal*. Good arenas support both real-time and time-delayed discussion. Real-time discussion allows people to interact dynamically, building on one another's ideas and opinions through back-and-forth dialogue—a kind of interchange that is particularly beneficial when brainstorming and exploring new concepts. Time-delayed discussion means that people interact progressively, with a time lag between discussion. This allows for more considered and thoughtful interaction, where participants have time to digest and ruminate on concepts, building on one another's thoughts before responding. Both real-time and time-delayed interactions are important and the best collaboration arenas cater to both to ensure that ideas emerge, evolve and coalesce in the most effective manner possible.

The second key attribute of a collaboration arena is *breadth of participation*, allowing for both group and individual interaction. Group interaction gives multiple people the opportunity to participate, either directly as a contributor or passively as an observer; even when a discussion is not of immediate relevance to a particular individual or organisation, being able to listen in means that awareness and understanding among all participants is continually elevated. Individual interaction allows sidebar conversations to develop that can address issues and ideas in greater detail; these are often pivotal in pushing an endeavour forward. It also provides a platform for conversations on topics that can't be brought to a larger group due to issues such as time restrictions or topic sensitivity.

After setting up the arena, the next aspect of a collaborative environment to consider is the **lexicon**. Most modern languages comprise around 150,000 words and most native speakers will recognise 15,000-20,000 of them.[14] Non-native speakers are generally thought to have achieved basic fluency when they have mastered 3,000 word groups. Unfortunately, as anybody who has ever tried to learn a foreign language knows, lots of words can have more than one meaning based on different circumstances. For example, in English, "*fast*" means to move quickly (move fast), to stand still (hold fast), to not eat (maintain a fast), or to not fade (colour-fast).

With idioms, buzzwords, acronyms and jargon becoming ever more prevalent, communication issues can arise quickly, even when people share a common language, culture and perspective. This is why it is so important to develop a lexicon for every collaborative endeavour—to both reduce the chances of misunderstanding *and* make communication more efficient and effective.

The lexicon isn't a dictionary. It doesn't record the meaning of every word used within the collaborative community—that would rapidly become a ridiculously unwieldy task. Instead, it clarifies terms and expressions that are particularly relevant and ensures that everybody has the same basic understanding of important words and expressions.

For most collaborative endeavours, the fastest and easiest way to develop a lexicon is to start with a general clarification of what is meant by some basic terms that are unique to that particular environment. Acronyms in particular are worth documenting because not everybody will be familiar with every acronym, and some may have a different understanding of them. For example, the acronym CBT has different meanings for people with backgrounds in educational systems, psychology or materials science.

Once an initial lexicon has been established, it can be augmented and refined over time. As new words and acronyms arise, they can be noted, defined, and placed within the lexicon. One particularly efficient way to grow the lexicon is to simply take note of every instance where confusion over a specific term arises, then agree the term's meaning within the context of the collaborative endeavour and add it to the lexicon.

The final critical aspect of a collaborative environment is a set of **guiding principles**. These are the standards that define how an endeavour functions—providing the basis for participants to understand what is generally expected of them and how they should operate. They are the fundamental rules of engagement and clarify the *how* rather than the *what* of the endeavour in both practical and philosophical terms. Although they are unique to every endeavour, there are some general categories that tend to be common.

Practical core principles define the operational aspects of collaboration such as:

- Accuracy tolerances.
- Measurement standards.
- Approved tools and processes.
- Standard formats.
- Communication protocols.
- Escalation procedures

Philosophical core principles define the ancillary aspects of collaboration such as:

- Honesty and transparency.
- Ethical standards
- Idea cultivation and nurturing.
- Issue reporting and problem management.
- Bureaucracy/administrivia reduction policies.
- Task ownership.

For a simple collaborative endeavour, the principles are usually relatively straightforward and concise. But, as the size and complexity of an endeavour increases, so too does the scope of the principles. For large endeavours with many moving parts and high participant numbers, the principles can become extensive. In effect, the endeavour becomes a mini-society that requires its own social standards. As with developing the lexicon, the best approach is to establish some initial principles, and then elaborate and expand them over time as new situations come to light that require clarification and definition.

Establishing guiding principles is the final component of constructing a functional collaborative community. But, as with other aspects of collaborative endeavours, rather than being an event, it's part of an iterative process that doesn't end until the endeavour has either achieved its purpose or failed. Most successful endeavours maintain stability throughout their lifecycle, but still require occasional adjustment and refinement. Collaborators drop out and have to be replaced, new capability requirements emerge that need to be satisfied, and collaboration arenas evolve to support the community in the most efficient and effective manner possible.

The Apollo Program

The United States made its first tentative steps in space exploration on 1 February 1958, three years before Kennedy suggested sending humans to the Moon. Unfortunately, it launched the Explorer 1 satellite four months after the Soviet Union had already entered the record books with Sputnik.[15]

Explorer I - Image courtesy: NASA

NASA formed a few months after the launch of Explorer 1, with a stated mission to "*provide for research into the problems of flight within and outside the Earth's atmosphere, and for other purposes*". But, the lack of clarity and focus of this broad mission probably contributed to the US losing out to the Soviet Union a second time three years later when Yuri Gagarin became the first human in space.

The fact that the US was so clearly losing the 'space race' was probably the motivation behind Kennedy's audacious suggestion to put a man on the Moon. He appears to have recognised that NASA had no clear direction, no definitive plans, and no unifying culture—something that he resolved in the twenty-five seconds that it took him to make his statement of purpose to the US Congress on 25 May 1961.

Kennedy's aspiration precipitated a science and engineering program unlike anything that had ever been seen before or, arguably, since. It was an endeavour on a grand scale, encompassing a huge network of participants with the collective experience, expertise and raw manpower to contribute to each of the missions that were steps along the way to a human walking on the Moon.

The list of groundbreaking capabilities that had to be harnessed was overwhelming: propulsion, navigation, guidance, telemetry, tracking, communications, data, planning, recovery, training, medicine, launch and life-support (food, air, heating, cooling, vehicles and suites). And these all had to be supported by administrative and support capabilities such as project management, human resources, public affairs, financial planning, building maintenance, legal affairs, office supplies, information technology and even sanitation. This multitude of skills, assets and experiences had to come together into a successful unified whole.

Some were certainly more significant and urgent than others, but absolutely none were irrelevant.

In achieving Kennedy's ambition, NASA effectively invented the modern-day procurement process. Organisations had contracted with third parties for specific products or services prior to the 1960s, but the sheer scale of procurement —or "acquisition" as it was referred to in NASA—for the US space program was beyond anything ever seen before. For each capability, NASA launched carefully managed initiatives and found willing and capable participants. Some were established organisations with extensive prior experience in an area while others had no pre-existing store of knowledge— often because nobody had ever previously conceived of a need for that capability. Some contractors were selected based on their track record, but others gained recognition because of a clear conviction that they could deliver a capability in time to contribute to the achievement of the purpose.

Competition was intense and participants worked hard to differentiate themselves. For example, one of the contractors, International Latex Corporation (ILC), recognised that mobility would be a defining feature in the design of the space suit to be used by astronauts on the Moon. It was already an experienced and respected expert in the design and manufacture of flight suits, but when it supported its bid with a movie of a man playing American football while wearing its proposed design for a lunar space suit, it moved from consideree to contractor.

ILC, like every other contractor, was assessed based on its individual merits and ability to contribute, but once integrated into the endeavour the ability to work well with others was also a key factor. NASA soon learned that operational disharmony was a serious barrier to success; with incredibly aggressive deadlines to meet, anything that potentially slowed progress was anathema to NASA leadership. When collaborators—individuals or organisations—didn't work together effectively, an inevitability from time to time, they were at risk of being sidelined in favour of others that were more team-oriented. NASA was very much a meritocracy where the individual or organisation with the best skills rose to the top; this meant that some level of prima donna behaviour was tolerated, albeit reluctantly. But, an ability to work well with others was highly valued and one of the key skills that contractors were expected to demonstrate. The 'best' participant was always the one who could deliver the required capability, but a willingness to also integrate within the collective was an attribute that frequently distinguished comparably qualified competing parties.

To support working together, collaboration environments were of paramount importance. The NASA headquarters in Washington DC was the 'centre of gravity' where leaders and administrators assembled to thrash out budgets and high-level plans that drove the various programs to ultimate success. But, critical work was conducted in locations across the United States. The Manned Spacecraft Center at Houston (for training, research and flight control) and the Launch Operations Center at Cape Canaveral (for vehicle assembly and launch) are probably the most famous, but there were many others. The Langley Research Center (for aeronautical research), the Ames Research Center (for aeronautics, spaceflight and IT) and the Marshall Space Flight Center (for rocket engines) were all instrumental in developing key aspects of the space program. In addition, there were private contractor and university locations all over the United States where teams came together to solve some of the most challenging science and engineering problems ever conceived.

In general, teams assembled physically, but NASA was also an early adopter of the virtual collaboration tools of the time.[16] It readily embraced the speakerphone—a revolutionary new technology that appeared in the late 1950s —as soon as it was readily available, and teams soon spent as much time discussing issues and ideas on teleconference lines as they did in physical rooms. NASA also took full advantage of emerging (predominantly mainframe computer based) messaging systems that began to emerge in the mid-1960s, sharing electronic files and notes between locations in seconds that would ordinarily take days.

In terms of a lexicon, the Apollo program overflowed with new words, expressions and acronyms. Scientists and engineers shared a common language in the form of mathematics, international standards and scientific notation, but the endeavour pushed human thinking to entirely new levels where effective communication wasn't just useful, it was essential. A great example of the new language that emerged during the space program was when Apollo 12 was struck by lightning, twice, shortly after take-off causing a worrying instrument malfunction. With an immediate understanding of what was happening, flight controller John Aaron made a single succinct recommendation, "*Flight, try SCE to AUX*". It was a brief but effective statement based on a common vocabulary that prevented an aborted mission; when the flight controller moved the signal conditioning equipment (SCE) to auxiliary mode (AUX) it did indeed resolve the issue.[17]

The Apollo program was also heavily dependent on extensive libraries of core principles. Some were philosophical, such as employees being empowered, and expected, to surface issues and concerns as soon as they came to light without fear of reprisal. Others were more practical, such as working to eight significant digits of pi,[18] which provided accuracy to 15 cm at 382,400 km—the distance of the Moon from the Earth.[19]

However, even with an emphasis on the establishment of unifying core principles, there were still examples of issues that arose because of different standards in different areas. A famous example is when the carbon dioxide scrubbers on the Apollo 13 Lunar Module became overwhelmed when it was being used as a 'lifeboat' during the emergency journey back to Earth. It was discovered that the obvious solution, replacing the Lunar Module scrubbers with those in the Command Module, wasn't possible because they were of a different size and shape. This forced the need to develop an equipment 'hack' in a limited time and with severely limited resources. A key lesson was learnt: whenever possible, design and build as many components as practicable to the same standards and specifications so that, if necessary, they can be *built once and used many times*—a concept now firmly entrenched not only in NASA core principles, but in general manufacturing principles everywhere.

The breadth and scale of the Apollo program was breathtaking. During the 1960s, NASA was the world's pre-eminent assembly of scientific and engineering minds, augmented by a huge network of support staff. At its height, it drew together over 400,000 people from 20,000 collaborative entities—public and private enterprises, research laboratories and universities—all working together towards a common purpose. Project Mercury (1958-63) sent the first American into space, Project Gemini (1961-66) established and tested the capabilities required to send humans to the Moon, and then finally on 20 July 1969, five months before the stated deadline of "the end of the decade", Project Apollo (1961-72) fulfilled the first part of Kennedy's vision to put a man on the Moon. A few days later it achieved the second part and returned them safely back to Earth.

NASA conducted five more manned missions to the Moon, finally ending with Apollo 17 in 1972. It's a testament to how incredibly difficult these collaborative endeavours were that in more than 50 years, humans still haven't returned in person.

Activate

> ### *To achieve ANY target outcome, inspiration and aspiration have to combine with perspiration and implementation*

Even the most well-crafted goals, by the most highly qualified community of collaborators, focused on a deeply engaging purpose, are still just theoretical aspirations. For *any* group or individual to achieve *any* outcome, ideas and intentions must be pushed from nebulous concept to practical reality.

And that is surprisingly difficult!

It's challenging to overcome inertia—the natural human tendency to do nothing, or at least do nothing too taxing. There are individuals who are high-performance exceptions, but given the choice most people take the less demanding road almost all of the time. The truth is, it's dangerously easy to get trapped in continual 'visioneering'—

dreaming about a target outcome, setting goals and talking, but not actually getting around to doing anything.

And this is true for collaborative endeavours! Even when participants are united by a common desire to achieve something. For small projects it's difficult to move from vision to action, but for larger, more challenging endeavours, the complexity of what must be accomplished and the magnitude of the target outcome can overwhelm even the most highly motivated of collaborative communities.

One way to break the inertia is to lay out what actually has to be done to achieve the target outcome. It's still *planning* rather than *doing*, but it's a more action-oriented form of planning that identifies specific actions—an important psychological nuance in the transition to implementation. When done effectively, the end product of action planning is a sequenced list of well-defined tasks that need to be undertaken to achieve a goal.

There are many ways of doing this, but one particularly effective technique is to develop ATA (approach/task/activity) networks—multi-layered roadmaps of the actions necessary to achieve each goal. These networks lay a strong foundation for momentum by overcoming blank page syndrome and exploring options to achieve goals, rather than just dreaming about them.

They're effective for almost any initiative, but are particularly well suited to collaborative endeavours where there are a lot of moving parts that must come together to achieve a target outcome—a feature that can prove intimidating when viewed at a high level. With ATA networks, actions are allocated owners and the orchestration and arrangement of effort between different participants becomes more obvious and manageable. They also support the powerful concept of micro-productivity, and break down large challenges into smaller steps that are considerably less daunting.

Another useful attribute of ATA networks is that they drive expansive thinking and encourage the exploration of a range of possible options to achieving goals. Rather than laying out a project plan of *definitive* actions that *must* be undertaken, they lay out lists of *possible* actions that *could* be undertaken. They not only move the participants in a collaborative community from nebulous ideas to tangible actions, but also provide a range of alternative actions that can feed backup plans and fallback options.

As with other processes associated with collaborative endeavours, an iterative approach is best and it isn't necessary to get too detailed during a first pass. In fact, it can be counter-productive to do so; it's better to remain at a high level and explore as many ideas as possible. Start by focusing on a goal and asking the question "*What approaches could be undertaken to achieve this?*" Occasionally, but rarely, there's only one feasible approach. Most of the time there are a handful that should be considered. Sometimes, there are a wide variety of options, some of which will have a greater chance of success than others.

CASE STUDY
The Tham Luang Non Cave Rescue

A great example of the value of considering multiple approaches during the early phases of a collaborative endeavour is the Tham Luang cave rescue.

The rescue was mounted when a group of twelve children—members of a Thai junior football team—and their coach, went missing on 23 June 2018. When some of the team's belongings were found at the entrance to the Tham Luang Nang Non cave, it was surmised that they had entered the cave that afternoon, shortly before a significant and unexpected rainstorm had flooded it.

The rescue operation grew quickly and within hours professional teams from around the world converged on the area. The Thai Navy SEALs, US Air Force, Australian Federal Police and Beijing Peaceland Foundation all sent teams and they immediately got to work searching the caves. But, a local cave specialist, Vern Unsworth, recognised that the rescue would require highly specialised expertise and experience, and suggested to the Thai government that the people to supply this were representatives of the British Cave Rescue Council (BCRC). After a few phone calls, BCRC members Richard Stanton, John Volanthen and Robert Harper were on their way. They landed on 27 June, and the very next morning—despite poor conditions—they entered the cave complex and began searching.

The initial search was, unsurprisingly, unsuccessful. But, undeterred and despite worsening conditions, teams of divers continued to penetrate deeper and deeper into the cave system, laying safety lines as they went. Then, on 2 July, with hopes fading, Rick Stanton and John Volanthen achieved the impossible and found the boys—nine days after they had disappeared and 2.5 km from the cave entrance. All twelve boys, and their coach, were alive and well—although understandably cold, tired, hungry and afraid.

From this point, the rescue operation moved into high gear. It has been estimated that at its peak, as many as 10,000 people were involved, including more than 100 divers—both general open water and specialist cave divers—using more than 700 dive tanks, of which 500 would be in the cave at any one time and the other 200 in a continuous queue to be refilled.

The operation had a range of possible approaches, but the six that gained the most traction were:

1. Do nothing until the end of the monsoon season and in the meantime use divers to ferry food and supplies to the group, with regular visits from rescue workers that would include medical doctors.
2. Locate and exploit another cave entrance as an alternative escape route.
3. Drill a rescue shaft from above through which the boys could be safely extracted.
4. Pump water out of the tunnel complex to the point that a non-submerged exit would be possible.
5. Utilise a mini 'sub' to bring out each boy, one at a time, over the space of several hours.
6. Bring the group out through the flooded tunnels using diving equipment with support from experienced cave rescue divers.
   a. Teach the group basic diving skills, and bring them out via a chain of experienced divers and other rescue workers.
   b. Anaesthetise each boy in turn and bring them out with one diver assigned per boy and a chain of support divers and rescue workers.

Approach 1 was the preferred option because it involved the least risk. But, it would mean that the group would be forced to remain in the cave for months since it would likely remain flooded until October or even November. However, it could be complemented by the simultaneous adoption of approaches 2, 3 and 4 in the (admittedly unlikely) hope that they would be successful and permit earlier rescue.

Approach 5 was a consideration, but deemed extremely difficult because some parts of the tunnel system were very narrow with extremely tight turns. The 'sub', which was really just a watertight rigid tube 170 cm long and 31 cm wide, would be unable to pass through it. For this to be a viable option either another route would have to be found, the tunnel would need to be widened, or the sub would need to be adapted to cope with the physical constraints of the tunnel system.

Approach 6 was of great interest, but with several very narrow tunnel sections, near-zero visibility, and areas of strong current flow, it would be hugely challenging. Approach 6a would require the boys to undertake a highly technical dive with a very real possibility that one of them would panic and put both themselves and their rescuers in peril. Approach 6b eliminated the danger of panic, but introduced different risks associated with long-duration sedation in a far from ideal environment.

It was the very fact that none of the approaches were discounted that created the foundation for ultimate success. Approach 1 may have been the preferred option, but the others were never rejected outright. Approaches 2, 3 and 4 were in continual operation with more than 100 shafts bored during the operation and a new natural tunnel discovered that went down to roughly the same vertical level as the boys, but was far too distant. Pumping water out of the tunnel was a never-ending exercise that was continued despite the fact that it was clearly a close-to-impossible option. Approach 5 wasn't fully discounted and, although low on the options list, a small team continued to brainstorm how a watertight escape canister might be brought into play. And, for approach 6, teams of rescuers were in the cave every hour, laying caches of ropes, harnesses, slings and specialist diving equipment along the entire length of the tunnel system. For each possible approach, rescue teams never stopped working out detailed action plans, including what needed to be done, when and how, so that if their approach became the preferred option, they would be ready to go.

As it turned out, the viability of approach 1 plummeted on day-13 of the endeavour when it was noticed that oxygen levels in the chamber where the boys were located were falling. By day-15, levels had dropped to just 15 percent and it became obvious that sitting it out until October was no longer a practicality. That was when focus shifted to approach 6—and then narrowed further to 6b.

On the morning of 8 July, the rescue team navigated the cave tunnels to the chamber in which the boys were located. Once there, Australian anaesthetist and experienced cave diver Dr Richard Harris carefully sedated the first four boys at 45-minute intervals before consecutively releasing each into the care of a rescue diver for the journey out of the tunnel. Jason Mallinson, Chris Jewell, John Volanthen and Richard Stanton then personally took one boy each through the tunnels—a journey of three hours—finally emerging in an area a few hundred metres from the cave entrance at which point a chain of over 200 people took over and transported each boy out and into a waiting ambulance. It is a testament to the skill, courage and logistical expertise of the rescue team that all four boys emerged from the cave system alive and in remarkably good health.

The following day, with conditions in the cave worsening and the weather deteriorating, another four boys were successfully evacuated, then finally on 10 July, the last four boys, along with their coach, were brought out, bringing to a conclusion one of the most technically challenging but brilliantly executed rescue operations of all time.

The Tham Luang rescue illustrates how it's possible to run multiple approaches simultaneously in pursuit of a goal, especially if they are complementary. For some endeavours this is warranted and it provides an element of redundancy so that if one approach fails, there are backup approaches immediately available. But, it has to be acknowledged that most collaborative endeavours have limitations in terms of both time and budget, and the luxury of maintaining multiple approaches in pursuit of the same goal is not possible: choices must be made. In these instances, the range of possible approaches needs to be pared down to those that are most appropriate for implementation.[20]

There are a variety of ways to do this. The ROSS technique is a simple approach and works well when dealing with long lists. The paired comparison approach is a little more involved, as every option must be compared with every other option, but it is commonly used and generally produces good results. And there are others too: the ABCDE method, the Eisenhower matrix and Kanban boards. All of these are valid, and all will result in a prioritised list of possible approaches for achieving a goal.

But, one particularly good technique for paring down options in a collaborative endeavour is to assess the risk versus the reward of different approaches. It's especially suitable because it tangibly focuses attention on the two most critical dimensions of an approach, and ensures that discussion centres around impact and outcome.

Of course, perceptions of risk and reward are subjective; what is acceptable for one group of people under one set of circumstances might be completely unacceptable to another. And, for some endeavours there may be goals where *all* possible approaches are high risk. These instances are unfortunate and disconcerting, but it doesn't really matter in terms of prioritisation. It's the relative risk—how the approaches compare to each other— that is important rather than the absolute risk. If, for example, all approaches are high risk, the objective is to differentiate between those that are the *highest* high risk and those that are *lower* high risk. What's of paramount importance is that the assessment is done consistently for all approaches.

For situations where the number of possible approaches is low and they're not hugely complex, the assessment can usually be accomplished as a general discussion around two core questions for each approach:

1) *If successful, how substantial will the benefit from this approach be and how much will it contribute to the overall achievement of the goal?*
2) *If unsuccessful, how severe will the consequences be from this approach and will it set back the overall achievement of the goal?*

The only complexity of paring down the options using this technique is in managing the discussion. Care must be taken to ensure that: (a) it doesn't drift off at tangents, (b) it doesn't get over-embroiled in details and sticking points, and (c) everybody has the opportunity to voice their opinion. A well-facilitated discussion should be able to reach consensus on which approach—or approaches—to undertake, and the most appropriate should rise to the surface during the conversation.

If it doesn't, perhaps because the possible approaches are more complex in nature, the discussion can be taken a little deeper. In these instances, the two core questions can be augmented with clarification questions.

For reward, clarification questions to consider are:

- *Will this approach spawn other opportunities and expand options, either now or in the future?*
- *Is this approach complementary with other approaches? Will it work in harmony with other actions and increase the ultimate chance of success?*
- *Can challenges associated with this approach be identified, mitigated, controlled and overcome?*
- *Will it be easy to access and control the assets (people, skills, resources) needed to undertake this approach?*

And for risk, clarification questions are:

- *Will this approach stifle or inhibit other opportunities, either now or in the future? Are short-term benefits offset by longer-term disadvantages?*
- *Is this approach in conflict with other approaches? Will it force a specific path of action to the exclusion of others?*
- *Are challenges associated with this approach especially difficult to predict, mitigate, control and overcome?*
- *Will it be difficult to access and control the assets (people, skills, resources) needed to undertake this approach?*

Although it may still be possible to reach consensus on which approach(es) to undertake simply by discussion, it's often better to codify the conversation. To do this, scores are assigned against each core question and its associated clarification questions, for example 0-9, A-E or even just high/medium/low. If necessary, perhaps because the debate is particularly contentious, each person can give a personal score to each question for each approach and these can be consolidated into overall group scores. The discussion can then be concluded by reviewing the results and selecting the approaches with the highest scores. This technique is particularly suitable when a group is finding it difficult to reach consensus because approaches have similar levels of risk or reward. It can break deadlock and has the added benefit of creating an at-a-glance record that can be referred to later to show how the group reached a decision.

There is a third variation to the risk/reward assessment that can be used when an endeavour has a wide variety of possible approaches. It follows the same general process of discussing the core questions together with clarification questions, but rather than apply scores to the answers, the conversation is distilled into risk and reward categorisations.

Suggested categories for reward are:

- **Limited**: completion of this approach could have a small positive impact on goal attainment.
- **Marginal**: completion of this approach could have a clear positive impact on goal attainment.
- **Beneficial**: completion of this approach could have a significant positive impact on goal attainment.
- **Invaluable**: completion of this approach could substantially improve the overall probability of goal attainment.

And for risk, suggested categories are:

- **Minimal**: failure to complete this approach could have a small negative impact on goal attainment.
- **Nominal**: failure to complete this approach could have a clear negative impact on goal attainment.
- **Consequential**: failure to complete this approach could have a far-reaching negative impact on goal attainment.
- **Perilous**: failure to complete this approach could have a catastrophic impact on goal attainment.

When all approaches have been assessed, they can be plotted onto a matrix that provides a visual representation of approach options and provides some useful default strategic conclusions.

The baseline interpretation is to focus on approaches that lie above a line of equilibrium that runs from the bottom

left of the model to the top right—approaches that are more
heavily biased towards reward. Beyond the baseline
interpretation, the goal should be to minimise approaches that
are high-risk/low-reward and maximise those that are low-
risk/high-reward.[21]

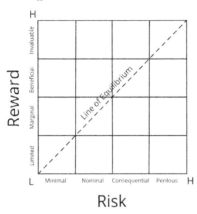

So, approaches
that fall into the bottom-
right and top-left
quadrants are relatively
easy, and obvious, to
interpret.[22] Approaches
that fall into the top-
right and bottom-left
quadrants are less clear-
cut, especially when the
risks and rewards are
evenly balanced. The
immediate conclusion,
for approaches in either
quadrant, is to avoid
except when there are compelling reasons to consider. For
those in the bottom-left, the most obvious compelling reason to
consider is if it would be relatively easy to undertake and have
a fast time-to-success. For approaches in the top-right
quadrant, the obvious compelling reason to consider is if the
rewards for success are exceptionally high or represent a major,
endeavour-defining step towards achieving the target
outcome.[23]

No matter what assessment technique is used, the
objective is to hone down the possible approaches to a small
number. Typically, a handful will stand out as being worthy of
consideration, and for most goals there will be one that stands
out as dominant—the primary approach—and two or three
that may be considered as possible secondary or backup
approaches. If the endeavour is fortunate enough to have
resources and finances available to undertake simultaneous
parallel approaches to achieving a goal, great. If not, the
primary approach is the one to take.

But, before auto-rejecting any secondary approaches,
it's advisable to make a first pass to think about what tasks
would be needed to undertake them. That way, there are
backup plans at least partially pre-developed in the instance
that the primary approach proves to be non-viable at a later

stage. It's acceptable to put all your eggs in one basket, and watch it very carefully, but it's less anxiety-inducing if there is another basket of eggs available … just in case.

The starting point for moving to the next level of the ATA network is to examine each viable approach and ask, *"What tasks must be undertaken to achieve this approach?"* As with any other brainstorming exercise, the process is to write down all of the possible answers—the tasks—then clarify, de-duplicate, and rationalise them. The final output will be a list of tasks that could be undertaken to achieve each approach.

There are three important subtleties to consider in task identification:

- First, it's acceptable for some tasks to be applicable to different approaches. In fact, it isn't unusual for more than half of the tasks for one approach to be fully applicable to another.
- Second, it isn't necessary to identify *all* required tasks in a first pass. As with other aspects of collaboration, task identification is an iterative process and not all tasks will be clear in the first iteration: sometimes, there will be several iterations before all of the tasks will be fully defined.
- Third, not all of the tasks will, or should, be marked for implementation. As mentioned earlier, ATA networks aren't restricted to identifying definitive actions, and some of the tasks identified will be *possible* actions that can be included in backup plans and kept as fallback options should other tasks fail.

Once the tasks that comprise an approach have been identified, the definition and sequencing process of preparing them for activation involves five steps.

The first is to **map interdependencies**—how

Approach Sequencing
Map Interdependencies
Overlay Time Constraints
Marshal Logistics
Clarify Ownership
Consider Risk

tasks are related to one another. This won't be relevant for every task, but it's common that an aspect of one has a bearing on another. The most obvious interdependence is start-to-finish, where the output from one task, or set of tasks, is the input for others. Clearly, these tasks have to be sequenced so that dependent tasks don't start until predecessor tasks are complete. But, this isn't the only relationship to consider and, although much rarer, other interdependencies are start-to-start (where two or more tasks should start simultaneously) and finish-to-finish (where tasks should finish simultaneously). While technically it's also possible for there to be a finish-to-start interdependence—where tasks should start before others finish—these are so rare as to be generally discountable as a consideration.

The second step is to **overlay time constraints**, such as specific dates by which tasks must be started or completed. Dependent on the endeavour, these can be based on any number of factors, such as market conditions, economic triggers, regulatory restrictions or even weather. Not every task will have them, in fact most won't, but those that do could have a direct impact on sequencing and success. It's not unknown for the viability of an entire approach—and therefore its parent goal—to be seriously undermined simply because a time constraint for a single task can't be easily accommodated. But, even this unfortunate situation is considerably better than the time constraint not being considered at all, and an entire endeavour failing when that later becomes apparent.

The third task definition and sequencing step is the most difficult of all—to **clarify and marshal the logistics** necessary to complete each task, such as human capital, raw materials, equipment, technology, tools, transportation and even finance. It's very common that tasks aren't specifically interdependent on one another in that the output of one task feeds the input for another, but are dependent because they require access to the same resources. When this is the case, a decision has to be made regarding which tasks to do first, and sequencing must be fine-tuned accordingly. It's a critical step because resource coordination across different tasks can have a profound impact on productivity, timelines and goal attainability.

The fourth step is **ownership clarification**— naming the individual or organisation responsible for ensuring that the task is completed on time and within budget. It's important to note that there is a small subtlety here that needs to be taken into account—that most of the time the task owner will also perform the work required to complete it, but not always. In some instances, the owner will be accountable for ensuring that the task is completed, but not necessarily commissioned with doing it, and will instead identify and supervise the effort of a third-party. So, it is the individual or group responsible for ensuring that the task is completed— whether or not they do the work—who should be included in the task definition.

Finally, the fifth step in task definition and sequencing is to **develop a risk assessment**, identifying any major threats that could adversely impact the completion of a task. Some risks will be relatively easy to identify—based on factors such as scarcity of resources or aggressive timing constraints. Other risks won't be so easily identified, and will be based on more unpredictable and unseen factors such as stakeholder dynamics, political upheaval or technological advances.

For all tasks, the objective is to identify as many risks as possible, and then to determine how they could be mitigated. For the sake of expediency, mitigation should be focused initially on the most likely threats. But, ultimately, all identified threats should at least be considered and, over time, mitigation plans expanded to include them. The ideal mitigation is to reduce the probability of a risk to zero. But, since this is not always possible, the minimum should be to outline supplementary actions that could minimise the severity of a threat in the instance that it materialises.[24]

For most collaborative endeavours task sequencing will need to be adjusted several times. Dependencies, time constraints and resource allocations in particular are tightly interlinked and changes in one area will drive movement in another. This can be further complicated when new tasks are identified and added into an ATA network. Adjustments will invariably have a ripple-through effect and it isn't unusual for a sequenced task list to be adjusted multiple times. Most task lists aren't truly complete until the endeavour itself is concluded.

The sequenced task list is a very strong driver for action and for many endeavours it will be enough to get moving. For others, it will be the foundation for a more rigorous project outline, and action won't start until associated plans and controlling mechanisms[25] have been put in place. For the most complex endeavours, it will be necessary to go even further and get to the third level of the ATA network— outlining the activities associated with each task. When this is necessary, the activities that comprise each task will also need to be outlined, defined and sequenced.

The most important thing to understand is that success for any project lies at the intersection of innovation and ideas with activity and execution. The reality is, lots of people have great ideas, but the true winners are those who are capable of bringing them to reality. Plans must be translated into tangible actions that move an endeavour towards the target outcome. And, to translate a plan into action, you need to start *doing*. ATA frameworks are a way to make the transition to action and to break down complex challenges into manageable components—something that is of particular importance to collaborative endeavours, where a range of activities will be undertaken in a coordinated manner by a variety of participants.

There's an old saying that "*a poor plan, well executed, is better than no plan at all*". It's a good philosophy and generally true. But, it's also true that "*an excellent plan never executed is of academic interest only*".

The most fundamental attribute of success for any endeavour is to do … something!

The Apollo Program

Unfortunately, although there is extensive preserved documentation for the Apollo program, there are no ATA networks. The teams responsible for the different aspects of the initiative were constantly faced with choices; approaches, tasks and activities were adjusted and

NASA Engineers - Image courtesy: NASA

refined on an ongoing basis. The sequenced task lists associated with any of the core goals of the Apollo program would probably amount to terabytes of data, and each task involved dozens—in some cases hundreds—of activities. Each activity had a comparable number of sub-activities, and all of these tasks and activities were interwoven with hundreds of thousands of others serving other goals.

As a very basic example, the core tasks needed to provide propulsion to get the Apollo spacecraft from the Earth to the Moon and back were:

a) Launch the spacecraft from the surface of the Earth into Earth orbit at a specific time, velocity, altitude and azimuth.

b) Transition the spacecraft from Earth orbit onto a trajectory towards the Moon.

c) Disengage the Command and Service Module (CSM) from the Saturn Stage 3 engine, rotate it 180 degrees, dock it with the Lunar Module (LM), and extract it from the Lunar Module Adapter Housing.

d) If required, perform up to four mid-course corrections during the journey to the Moon.

e) Transition the spacecraft into lunar orbit at an appropriate time, velocity, altitude and azimuth.

f) Separate the Lunar Module from the Command and Service Module before moving it into a controlled descent to land on the lunar surface, allowing for manual adjustments as required during descent.

g) Maintain the Command and Service Module in lunar orbit.

h) After lunar exploration, launch the Lunar Module from the Moon surface back to lunar orbit at an appropriate time, velocity, altitude and azimuth to re-engage with the Command and Service Module, allowing the Lunar Module crew to re-enter the Command and Service Module.

i) Separate the Command and Service Module from the Lunar Module, abandoning the latter.

j) Transition the Command and Service Module from lunar orbit onto a trajectory towards Earth.

k) If required, perform up to four mid-course corrections during the journey back to Earth.

l) Transition the Command and Service Module trajectory to one that enables re-entry at a specific time, velocity, distance and azimuth.

m) Separate the Command Module (CM) from the Service Module (SM).

n) Make required adjustments to fine-tune the Command Module trajectory for re-entry and subsequent splashdown at a pre-defined location, accurate to within 3 km.

There was probably no attempt to develop any kind of risk/reward model for these tasks. For each task, the reward was high. The goal of propulsion simply could not be accomplished without them. But, the risks were similarly high; if any one task was not accomplished, the goal would not be reached. While there were backup options, these were far from ideal, and during some stages of the mission there really were no alternatives other than success.

The level of difficulty in achieving these tasks, and the complexity of the activities necessary to activate them, cannot be understated. For example, looking at just the first task—getting the spacecraft into Earth orbit and then on a path towards the Moon—required 35,000 metric tons of thrust and involved accelerating to a speed of 40,000 kmh. At that time, rocket science was around 20 years old and this was pushing it to boundaries beyond anything previously conceived. In terms of fuel alone, it required the safe storage of 800,000 litres of kerosene, 950,000 litres of liquid hydrogen and 1.5 million litres of liquid oxygen, which could then be burnt at a precisely controlled rate through heat-resistant nozzles fitted with gimbals to deliver vectored thrust to accurately position the vehicle in three-dimensional space.

The complexity associated with just storing that amount of explosive fuel was staggering, let alone finding a way to safely burn it!

Another great example of the complexity of the task lists for the Apollo program is the lunar space suit. The initial list of tasks that had to be achieved included:

a) Allowing (unpressurised) wear during all Apollo mission phases.
b) Providing backup short-term emergency protection in the event of spacecraft failures.
c) Supporting a range of mobility that allows not only entry and exit to/from the Lunar Module and exploration of the surface of the Moon, but also operation of a spacecraft (Command Module and/or Lunar Module) during unscheduled cabin pressure-loss events including, if necessary, a 115-hour transit period from the lunar surface to Earth's atmosphere in the event of spacecraft decompression.
d) Ensuring durability that allows for, as a minimum, the user to fall on the surface of the Moon, against rocks, without compromising the overall integrity of the system.
e) Protecting against micro-meteoroids of up to 0.24 cm in diameter, 3.5 g/cm^3 in density and moving at 0.2 km/s (~500 mph).
f) Providing up to 450 minutes of self-contained use, allowing Moon walks of up to 7 hours.
g) Delivering thermal protection in the instance of a spacecraft fire of up to 650 C.

It's worth noting that none of these tasks were easy, but satisfying them while still allowing a reasonable amount of movement was something that dramatically increased the difficulty of them all. Creating a suit that could provide all of the required protection for a man to stand on the incredibly inhospitable surface of the Moon[26] was difficult enough; achieving this while also allowing the user to move around, use equipment, and kneel was an enormous additional step.

And, breaking down the tasks into a defined and sequenced list of activities, and the activities into defined and sequenced sub-activities, was absolutely essential for the development of the space suit. Although it's generally thought of as a major achievement of International Latex

Corporation, it was actually the product of a long list of participants, each of whom took responsibility for one particular area—and in some instances just one activity. A partial list of the collaborators is:

- Pressure suit: developed by International Latex Corporation (ILC).
- Portable Life Support Assembly (aka the backpack): developed by the Hamilton Standard Division (HSD) of United Aircraft and David Clark Company (DCC).
- Lunar Extravehicular Visor Assembly: developed by Perkins Elmer Corporation (gold coating) and HSD with support from NASA directly,[27] Air-Lock Corporation (A-L) and ILC.
- Integrated Thermal Outer Gloves: developed by DCC and ILC.
- Torso Thermal Meteoroid Garment: developed by DCC and ILC.
- Extra-Vehicular Over Boots: developed by DCC and ILC.
- Primary Life Support System: developed by HSD.
- Oxygen Purge System: developed by HSD.
- Remote Control Unit (chest mounted display and control system for the backpack): developed by HSD.
- Life Support Connectors: developed by A-L and DCC.
- Moulded Convolute Joint: developed by B.F. Goodrich (BFG) and ILC.
- Moulded Pressure Gloves: developed by ILC, but drawing heavily on previous designs from BFG and incorporating concepts developed by HSD.
- Shoulder Cable Restraints: developed by ILC, but based on initial designs by HSD.
- Pressure (Lip) Sealed Upper Arm Bearings: developed by ILC and A-L, but based on early designs by BFG and HSD.
- Shoulder Teflon Ferrule Multi-Direction Joint: developed by ILC (based on pre-existing technology).
- Apollo Walking Brief: developed by ILC (based on pre-existing technology).
- Bubble Helmet: developed by A-L.
- Helmet Visor: developed by American Optical Corporation.
- Anti-Scratch Visor Coating: developed by Foster Grant.

- Liquid Cooled Garment & Multiple Water Connector: developed by A-L, but based on a design by HSD.
- Helmet Drink Port: internally developed by NASA.
- Walking Ankle Joint: developed by HSD.
- Rear Entry System: developed by ILC, but based on concept designs from DCC.
- Pressure Sealing Zipper: developed by BFG.
- Helmet Vent Duct: internally developed by NASA.
- Urine Collection and Transfer Assembly: developed by BFG.
- Injection Patch: developed by DCC.
- Communication Antennae System: developed by Stanley Tools Corporation.

It's an impressive list, and orchestrating the multitude of activities that all of these organisations had to deliver to produce an amazing unified solution was an incredible achievement. The final product—although it's probably best described as a system—was a true marvel of ergonomic design and engineering. It's a testament to just how well designed the system was that it continued to be the primary Extravehicular Mobility Unit used by NASA, with enhancements and modifications, right up until 1992.

Evaluate

> ## *To navigate from A to B you need to know your speed, direction and fuel reserves*

The statement "*if you can't measure it, you can't manage it*"[28] isn't always true in all situations, but it is mostly true in most situations. And it's certainly easier to manage an activity that is effectively measured[29] than one that is not. This is especially true for collaborative endeavours where the tasks and activities to be accomplished are undertaken by a diverse group of participants from different backgrounds with a wide range of interests and motivations. Often, they also have other commitments competing for their time and attention, and can be based in broadly separated geographic locations.

In such complex environments, it's challenging to maintain an understanding of how the endeavour is moving towards completion. The only truly effective way is by continuously evaluating progress, and that means answering two primary questions:

1) *Is the endeavour proceeding as expected?*
2) *Are participants fully engaged in it?*

When combined, the answers indicate whether or not the endeavour is on track and, perhaps more importantly, if it is likely to remain on track and go on to achieve the target outcome.[30] The answers also provide early warning indicators of areas for concern—in the process ensuring that minor (solvable) issues are discovered before they evolve into major (intractable) problems.

The first question is focused on operational metrics that typically fall into five major categories:

- **Schedule**: looks at how the endeavour is running according to timing expectations—reviewing milestones and deliverables and assessing if they are being reached on time.
- **Financials**: examines the economics associated with the endeavour—monitoring spending and/or income and comparing them to financial projections.
- **Quality**: focuses on the general functionality of deliverables produced by the endeavour—measuring if output is meeting anticipated standards.
- **Resource Utilisation**: focuses on equipment and supplies—assessing if they are being utilised effectively and at planned rates of consumption.
- **Effort**: considers the human dynamics of the endeavour—evaluating if levels of individual and team effort are appropriate and sustainable.

For relatively simple endeavours it is usually sufficient to make a qualitative assessment at the endeavour level with a RAG report. A simple red/amber/green evaluation is made for each category from the overall perspective of the endeavour. Green indicates progress is as expected with no perceived areas of concern, amber indicates some issues or concerns, but none that threaten overall success, and red indicates significant issues that could pose a tangible threat to the endeavour. If useful, a fourth, blue category can be added for when an endeavour is exceeding expectations within a category and—at the other end of the spectrum—a fifth, black category for when there are issues within a category that pose a clear existential threat, and must be addressed immediately.

For some endeavours, a goal-level assessment will be acceptable—assessing each goal against the five categories—but for others it might be necessary to get down to the approach and task level.

			Schedule	Financials	Quality	Resource Utilisation	Effort
Goal-1	Approach-1.1	Task-1.1.1					
		Task-1.1.2					
		Task-1.1.3					
		Task-1.1.4					
	Approach-1.2	Task-1.2.1					
		Task-1.2.2					
Goal-2	Approach-2.1	Task-2.1.1					
		Task-2.1.2					
	Approach-2.2	Task-2.2.1					
		Task-2.2.2					
	Approach-2.3	Task-2.3.1					
Goal-3	Approach-3.1	Task-3.1.1					
		Task-3.1.2					
		Task-3.1.3					
		Task-3.1.4					
		Task-3.1.5					
Goal-4	Approach-4.1	Task-4.1.1					
		Task-4.1.2					
		Task-4.1.3					
		Task-4.1.4					
	Approach-4.2	Task-4.2.1					

Occasionally, it will be necessary to get all the way down to the individual activity level. And, instead of a broad qualitative assessment, it may be necessary to conduct a more quantitative assessment based on key performance indicators[31] that are indicative of a particular operational category. What key performance indicators to use will be different for every endeavour but, for example, indicators for the 'schedule' category could be: percentage action complete, milestone variance, action lead time, action cycle time and issue resolution time.

No matter the level, regularly revisiting the evaluation and updating the RAG report(s) provides a continual assessment of operational performance and helps focus attention on areas where there may be a need for greater focus, or even the activation of backup plans.[32]

But, it's important to understand that, although it may be possible to get down to a highly granular level of evaluation, this isn't necessarily desirable. In some instances it can actually be *undesirable*. Collaborative evaluation should be undertaken at the highest practical level that still allows a clear understanding of progress. That's because over-measurement is every bit as insidious as under-measurement; it consumes valuable effort and frustrates those participants who have a natural bias towards action. Instead of pushing forward with tasks and activities, time and effort is expended on measurement.

Good evaluation requires an appropriate, not overwhelming, amount of data that is both easy to capture and easy to interpret. The goal is to achieve a balanced simplicity —enough information to be able to effectively manage the endeavour with early warning of issues while not burying participants in requests for information and progress reports. There are no hard and fast rules, and every endeavour is different, but in general if evaluation activities are consuming more than ten percent of the total effort for an endeavour, it's probably too much. If they are consuming more than twenty percent of effort, it's DEFINITELY too much.

Over-measurement can confuse as much as clarify. When there is an excess of metrics, they can be increasingly difficult to understand, and this leads to an opaque view in which issues can go unnoticed and unaddressed. In the worst-case scenario, a phenomenon known as the 'watermelon effect' arises where there are lots of metrics, most of which show as green, giving an overall impression of an endeavour on track. However, the expansive layer of green masks the fact that beneath the surface there are amber or red issues that need to be dealt with.[33] When the watermelon effect is particularly acute, serious issues are completely overlooked until they become impossible to ignore—by which time they are a tangible and potentially insurmountable threat to the success of an endeavour.

| CASE STUDY |
| The Subprime Mortgage Crisis |

The subprime mortgage crisis, is an excellent example of this. It originated in the United States in 2001 but the effects were felt around the world. The genesis was the bursting of the dot-com bubble (leading to a decline of the NASDAQ stock exchange) combined with a fall in GDP and a rise in unemployment. The US central bank (known as the Federal Reserve), staffed by people with limited imagination and creativity, did what central banks always do in such situations: lowered interest rates.

The new low-interest rates did what they always do and triggered a growth in house buying that led to a corresponding growth in mortgage debt. This in itself wasn't a bad thing; after all, home ownership was the dream of a significant proportion of the US population and helping people realise that dream was generally viewed as a positive move. The problem was that mortgage providers began lending money to amateur property speculators looking to take advantage of the property boom and to people who didn't have strong financial stability.

Almost immediately, the first of three key metrics—the ratio of US household debt to personal income—started moving into the red zone. It was 99.9 percent in 2000, 103.4 percent in 2001 and 108.7 percent in 2002.

But, things were set to go from bad to worse. Mortgage lenders weren't the only group capitalising on the housing boom: the investment banks saw an opportunity too. Unlike the Federal Reserve, they are populated by people with excellent imagination and creativity, and after purchasing mortgages from mortgage providers, including subprime mortgages, they 'securitised them' into exotic financial instruments known as mortgage backed securities (MBS's)—effectively, groups of mortgages pooled together as a single investment that could be bought and sold on the open market. They even grouped MBS's into extended securities—collateralised debt obligations, or CDO's—that could be further sliced up into tranches according to level of risk.

The core concept was that if some of the mortgages failed in some of the MBS's (or CDO's), it would be acceptable because the majority would remain active and viable. In such instances, the high-risk tranches (known as juniors) would provide low return, but the lower-risk tranches (known as seniors) would be okay. Credit rating agencies fully bought into the concept and, as trading in MBS's and CDO's exploded, gave them a firm stamp of approval.

Global investors flocked to the market, prices climbed and all of the metrics showed nothing but green. Charts and tables covering data such as trading volumes, investor interest, prices, yields, earnings and dividends were all positive. But, the performance data was not representative of the mortgages that comprised those securities. In fact, they were completely misleading. The investment banks knew this, and many of the mortgage providers knew it too, but since they were all making massive amounts of money they chose to ignore it and continue to line their pockets.

Unfortunately, the less financially astute people at the Federal Reserve didn't know it, didn't understand it or, most likely, weren't looking at the data at all. What they were looking at were macro indicators that showed inflation creeping upwards and a danger of economic overheating. So, they once again pulled the only lever that they knew how to operate: interest rates. They raised them 0.25 percent in June of 2004, and when that had no effect, raised them another 0.25 percent in August, and then another 0.25 percent in September. With inflation stubbornly refusing to react, they kept on raising interest rates by roughly a quarter of a percent each month so that, by the middle of 2006, interest rates were at 5.25 percent: up from 1 percent in June 2003.

By now, alarm bells should have been ringing in the Federal Reserve. That critical metric of household debt to personal income had climbed to 135.29 percent, and two other critical metrics were moving too—house prices and mortgage defaults. With a quintupling of interest rates in just three years, house prices fell as prospective home owners realised that mortgages were no longer within their financial means. At the same time, existing home holders struggled to meet mortgage payments and defaults began to climb: 1.59 percent in mid-2005; 1.74 percent in mid-2006; 2.71 percent in mid-2007; 5.28 percent in mid-2008.[34]

But, although the metrics were clear for everybody to see, and some financial analysts were expressing concerns, the markets generally ignored them. The Federal Reserve, in a breathtaking display of incompetence, did nothing. As the meltdown approached with horrible inevitability, the central bank showed how little it knew about modern financial systems and completely failed to recognise the ramifications of its unforgivably blunt approach to fiscal policy.

But the rest of the world woke up.

In July 2007, investment bank Bear Stearns announced the demise of two of its hedge funds that had invested heavily in securities derived from mortgages. Suddenly, the metrics on the trading screens of investment banks went from green to red as investors took a hard look at the metrics behind the numbers and saw the worrying signs of a developing mortgage crisis. Interest in MBS's and CDO's evaporated overnight, and the markets imploded. Lehman Brothers followed Bear Stearns into financial ruin and the contagion spread across Wall Street and around the world. As

2007 progressed into 2008, global stock markets stalled,
financial institutions crumbled and the Great Recession of
2008 arrived.

There's a lot of blame to go around for the subprime
mortgage crisis: unscrupulous mortgage providers who offered
loans to people who would struggle to meet monthly
payments; duplicitous investment banks, who purchased then
pooled mortgages into exotic financial instruments before
slicing and dicing them into even more exotic financial
instruments so that their (questionable) value could be
obscured; inept credit agencies that had neither the desire nor
the acumen to fully analyse the debt pools that comprised the
securities created by the investment banks and, instead,
charged handsome fees for triple-A credit ratings; and, most of
all, the Federal Reserve that demonstrated an astounding
incompetence in monetary policy and a total lack of oversight
and understanding of the US financial system. Instead of
closely monitoring critical key metrics like household debt to
personal income ratios, or residential house price movement
and residential and commercial mortgage defaults, they were
focused on blunt macro indicators such as GDP, inflation,
consumption and global trade. They were oblivious to the
catastrophe they were creating until it was too late.

The subprime crisis is an excellent example of
focusing on the wrong metrics and missing underlying issues.
But, even in more general terms there are two very common
situations on collaborative endeavours where metrics can
obscure rather than illuminate issues.

The first is when most indicators are showing green
with the exception of budget. Minor budget variances can be
tolerated occasionally but will rarely be acceptable on a long-
term basis, and endeavours that show even small—seemingly
insignificant—budget problems usually have a steadily
diminishing probability of success. At some point,
stakeholders will recognise that their investment is at threat
and will withdraw access to funds. The second situation is
even more dangerous as it can be especially hard to spot—
when all indicators show green with the exception of
participant effort, which is higher than planned or expected.
Once again, this can be acceptable for a while, but if the effort
required for an endeavour is especially high for some

participants, this is impossible to maintain in the long term. Endeavours that are dependent on relentlessly heroic effort are ultimately failures waiting to happen.

And, this is one of the reasons that, despite often being overlooked, it's also important to examine behavioural performance in addition to operational performance. Where operational performance evaluation is conducted at the approach, task or activity level, behavioural performance evaluation is performed at the community, team or individual level and answers the second question mentioned earlier: "*Are participants fully engaged in the endeavour?*" This gauges the general health of the collaborative community and takes a more aetiological[35] view, looking at whether or not participants are committed to the endeavour and continue to believe in the target outcome?

As with most assessments involving people, behavioural evaluation is a less definitive exercise and often requires a more subtle approach. It isn't always immediately obvious how engaged people are and their level of enthusiasm often has to be inferred from indirect observations in three areas:

- **Contribution**: examines involvement in the endeavour, and tests if participants' actions are meeting, missing, or exceeding expectations[36]—reviewing input, involvement, accountability and impact. It investigates if participants are showing up and delivering on their responsibilities.
- **Communication**: looks at how effectively participants are talking to one another—measuring if communication channels are open, transparent and free flowing. It monitors if participants are operating openly and honestly with no barriers or filters to issues or concerns.
- **Confidence**: considers the general level of participant enthusiasm and optimism—evaluating overall belief that the ultimate outcome of the endeavour is achievable and worthwhile. It looks at how positive participants are about the target outcome and if they demonstrate a belief that it will be achieved.

Behavioural evaluation can be done at the community level—looking across the endeavour as a whole and evaluating progress generally for all participants. This will be adequate for some endeavours, but it is usually necessary to get a little more detailed, at least down to the team level. For some endeavours, it will be worthwhile to go all the way down to the individual participant level.

No matter what level is adopted, just as with the operational evaluation, areas assessed as amber (some issues or concerns) should be closely monitored, and those assessed as red (significant issues or concerns) should become areas of focus. The importance of rapid reaction to behavioural evaluation issues cannot be overstated, because even a very small drop in participant engagement can rapidly devastate a collaborative endeavour.

One way to optimise behavioural evaluation, and in the process reduce over-measurement, is to sample key metrics occasionally but monitor a macro evaluator on a more frequent or even continual basis. If the macro evaluator indicates no cause for concern, the more detailed metrics can be deprioritised. But, if the macro evaluator changes, the more detailed metrics should be brought to the fore and examined more closely to better understand what could be happening.

Net Engagement Score

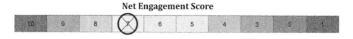

An excellent macro evaluator for collaborative endeavours is the Net Engagement Score™ (NES), which is based on participant responses to a single pivotal question "*How do you perceive the progress of the endeavour?*" Sometimes this can be a regular but relatively informal process, with senior participants in the endeavour asking the question of participants with whom they are working and then feeding this back. While not giving a definitive assessment, this does allow for some level of 'keeping a finger on the pulse' of the endeavour. A more detailed quantitative approach is to ask all participants—or at the minimum an appropriate representative sample of participants—to assign a score from 1 to 10 to the question. This offers much deeper insights and a more refined overall perspective.

The absolute value of the NES provides some insight into the general health of an endeavour, with high numbers indicating strong engagement, and low scores suggesting the opposite. But, what qualifies as a good score can vary widely depending on the nature and context of the endeavour. For example, a score of 7.3 might be considered excellent for some endeavours, but only acceptable for others. This variability is down to a variety of factors such as the maturity and seniority of the participants—more senior people tend to score more conservatively—or cultural differences, with different social groups having different perceptions of what is an average, good or excellent score.

So, it's important to establish a baseline as early as possible, and then monitor how it evolves over time. Rather than fixating on the absolute number, it's more informative to observe how it changes over time. As might be expected, a rising NES score generally indicates increasing engagement while a falling score suggests a decline—although these interpretations aren't guaranteed because group dynamics have an impact. For example, as groups move through different phases of maturity, the score will naturally fluctuate. In the very early phases of an endeavour, enthusiasm and engagement are typically high, but they usually fall a little as work progresses. In such situations, a shallow decline in NES score isn't any cause for alarm and simply reflects that the group is moving through a transitionary period. But, when scores drop rapidly and unexpectedly there is almost certainly a problem and further information, coupled with decisive action, is needed.

The same is true for relative NES scores between different participant groups within an endeavour. One group of participants may be facing significant challenges while another is in a breakthrough phase and making strong progress. It's only to be expected that the scores would be different for both teams. However, there are interesting psychological concepts to bear in mind here. For example, challenging periods and complex problem solving do not necessarily lead to decreasing NES scores. In fact, manageable adversity often bolsters engagement, particularly when teams are confident in their abilities to overcome obstacles. In the same vein, low-stress business-as-usual situations don't necessarily result in rising NES scores and it's more common for scores to fall during periods where progress is stable but mundane.

So, the trick when monitoring and assessing NES scores is to treat it as longitudinal data—looking at how relative scores, across the entire endeavour, are evolving over time. If scores remain consistent, it's reasonably safe to assume that the endeavour is stable and proceeding generally as expected. In such situations, there isn't a pressing need for a deeper dive into more detailed behavioural metrics. But, fluctuating scores—and especially steep declines—are early warning signs that further investigation should be done to understand what is behind the numbers, and what should be done to address any emerging issues.

Overall, the significance of evaluation in collaborative endeavours cannot be overstated. It illuminates the path to success and is an essential aspect of navigating the complexities of what is required to achieve a target outcome. It helps identify challenges as they emerge rather than when they are established, so that they can be addressed before they push an endeavour off track. It also fosters a culture of accountability and continuous improvement whereby individuals and groups within the community can be held accountable for their contributions, thereby deepening ownership.[37] Evaluation should never be the most laborious aspect of an endeavour, but it should always be a central point around which other effort revolves.

The Apollo Program

Right from the start, NASA had strong program and project management skills, with many of the early staff bringing extensive experience of complex initiatives from a wide range of public, private and educational sectors. During its first few years, it further developed those capabilities and as the Mercury, Gemini and Apollo programs progressed, NASA refined and updated both its expertise and approach.

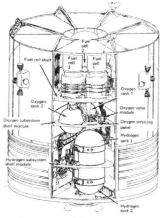

Apollo Service Module - Image courtesy: NASA

In July 1963, when George E. Mueller was appointed as Deputy Associate Administrator for Manned Space Flight, the agency was restructured so that Robert Gilruth (the head of the Manned Spacecraft Center), Werner von Braun (the head of the Marshall Space Flight Center), and Kurt Debus (the head of the Launch Operations Center) all reported to him. This new organisational model ensured that Mueller had the responsibility and the authority to centrally manage almost every aspect of the Apollo program.

Mueller was a consummate program manager, and there is no question that his approach was effective; after all, it succeeded in realising Kennedy's audacious vision to place a man on the Moon and return him safely back to Earth before the end of the decade. But, evaluation was one of the areas where there were occasional miscues. The stumbles weren't associated with what was evaluated, how evaluations were interpreted, or how evaluation data was acted upon; rather, they were associated with the sheer volume of evaluation that was required of everybody associated with the initiative.

Priorities defined how evaluation was treated across the organisation, with timeline, quality and budget being the mainstay of reporting. NASA expected extremely detailed reports on a frequent, sometimes daily, basis that outlined progress down to the finest of details. The result was a volume of data, both from external contractors and internal NASA departments, that was huge. It was a major source of frustration and concern across the organisation and a common area for complaint and criticism. Even Werner von Braun found it exasperating and was famously quoted in the Chicago Sun Times as saying *"we can lick gravity, but sometimes the paperwork is overwhelming"*.

For example, one of the ways that NASA over-administered evaluation was the establishment of formalised interfaces with contractors. NASA staff were placed as Resident Managers (RMs) at contractor locations. Unsurprisingly, this caused friction, since contractors were unaccustomed to having customer staff on-site, looking over their shoulders and monitoring progress on a real-time basis. Resident Managers found themselves in an exceptionally challenging position, with contractors seeing them as spies in their midst and their NASA colleagues seeing them as overly supportive contractor advocates. They had to be ultra-sensitive to not overstepping their mark while also maintaining understanding of the deliverables for which they had oversight. It became especially challenging when evaluation requests passed to them for cascade required extensive time and effort that detracted from getting the job done.

The fact that there was too much evaluation on the Apollo program isn't really questioned; it's been highlighted in numerous reviews of NASA policies and procedures from that time. The burden of providing a constant stream of reports was overwhelming, and there are examples of where too much evaluation probably obscured important and pertinent issues that went unaddressed. One example is with the #2 oxygen tank on the Apollo 13 spacecraft.

The oxygen tank was originally intended to be used on the Apollo 10 spacecraft, but a few weeks prior to launch, it was dropped by around six centimetres while being serviced, marginally damaging an internal fill line. The tank was visually inspected and didn't show any obvious signs of damage, but because of time pressures and an abundance of caution, it was replaced with another tank prior to launch. The seemingly minor event was noted, reported and filed— along with thousands of other required maintenance reports.

In the buildup to the Apollo 13 launch, oxygen tank #2 showed some anomalies and in particular would not empty correctly. But, engineers used the internal tank heater to boil off the excess oxygen and everything seemed fine. However, this turned out to be the root cause of the problems that astronauts Lovell, Swigert and Haise subsequently had to deal with while en route to the Moon.

The problem was that the tank was originally designed to run off the 28V DC power supplied by the Command and Service Modules, but was later upgraded to also run off 65V DC ground power while at the Kennedy Space Center. All components were upgraded with the exception of the internal thermostatic switches, which were overlooked. When the engineers working on Apollo 13 pre-flight boiled off excess oxygen in the tank, the thermostatic switches overloaded, welded shut, and temperature rose to over 500 C. The gauges only measured up to 25 C so the extreme heat wasn't noticed as it seriously damaged the Teflon insulation on the electrical wires to the power fans within the tank.

Unfortunately, despite multiple reports and data that should have prompted concerns—but instead obscured them —the damage to the insulation on the wires didn't become apparent until 56 hours into the flight of Apollo 13 when John "Jack" Swigert 'stirred' oxygen tank #2—a routine task intended to prevent the ultra-cold gas from stratifying into layers. As soon as he flipped the switch to perform the task, the exposed fan wires shorted, the Teflon insulation ignited, the pressure inside the tank rose, the electrical conduit on the side of the tank weakened and ruptured, and the tank exploded—in the process also damaging the #1 tank and parts of the interior and exterior of the Service Module.

It's arguable whether the damage to the Apollo 13 #2 oxygen tank would have been noticed if better evaluation processes were being observed. Maybe not. But, there's no debate that NASA was drowning in evaluation data, and small issues were very easy to miss because of the sheer volume of reporting.

In its defence, it has to be pointed out that the Apollo program was pushing the frontiers of science and engineering to achieve something of truly incredible difficulty. It's completely understandable that NASA over-evaluated given that the stakes were so high. In general, evaluation was well conducted and problems were identified early and addressed quickly. Also, as issues were identified, they were 'projectized',[38] a NASA expression for assembling task forces to rapidly resolve problems as they arose. NASA was making up the rules as it went along and there were understandable, occasional bumps in the road—some of them fatal. But 99.99 percent of the time, NASA got it right.

Motivate

> ## To climb any mountain, you've got to want to climb it

Motivation is one of the more psychologically complex aspects of collaborative endeavours. Assembling a group of people into a community is never easy and there are always other responsibilities competing for participants' time and attention. If collective motivation wavers, collaborative communities fall apart quickly. One moment the group is forging ahead towards achieving its target purpose, and the next, it's all over.

So, it's crucial to maintain motivation across the community, at both individual and collective levels. It's the indispensable unseen force that binds participants together while simultaneously driving the endeavour forward through the various stages of maturity that define group activities— from initial formation to final dissolution.

Most people are familiar with Bruce Tuckman's stages of group development theory, but it's worth looking at it within the specific context of a collaborative endeavour:

- **Forming:** when a collaborative community comes together and coalesces around a defined purpose. During this stage, relationships are formed and everybody is on their best behaviour while orienting themselves

> **Tuckman Stages of Group Development**
>
> Forming
> Storming
> Norming
> Performing

to individual and group responsibilities. Motivation is typically high, but tempered by some scepticism around the target outcome or its attainability.

- **Storming:** group dynamics stabilise as an organisational structure takes shape and relationships solidify. During this stage, ideas and opinions begin to emerge, leading to early momentum but also potentially fomenting conflict. Disagreements and personality clashes are possible as people begin to push boundaries.[39] This is one of the more vulnerable stages of an endeavour as people begin to come to terms with what is needed to achieve the purpose. Some participants may drop out and need to be replaced, but community adjustments can't be allowed to undermine the collective shared vision.

- **Norming:** the community establishes clarity of purpose and action while relationships deepen and esprit de corps grows. During this stage, participants fully understand their role and responsibilities and some may even embrace additional responsibilities beyond their initial commitments. Motivation is usually stable but must be carefully managed when inevitable, unforeseen obstacles appear that can tarnish enthusiasm and interest.

- **Performing:** the group establishes clear focus on achieving the purpose of the endeavour. Group commitment is high and interaction is predominantly productive. Disagreement and debate may still be present, but managed and coordinated so that they drive continual improvement rather than philosophical divergence. Motivation is high and participants typically have a strong sense of collective responsibility. Although the target outcome, as defined by the statement of purpose, isn't necessarily within sight, the path to achieving it is clear in the minds of the majority of participants.

Of course, collaborative communities rarely move in a steady linear fashion through the various stages of group development. It's much more common for them to bounce and jump around on the road to maturity. Most will pass through each of the developmental stages, but will move through some of them faster than others, and occasionally multiple times. It isn't unusual for a community to progress all the way to performing, only to have something change and cause a reversion all the way back to forming. There can also be some parts of the community operating in one stage while other parts are in other stages. These changes in group dynamics mean that the intensity of motivation also varies at both group and individual levels.

This is why it's so important to continually evaluate performance and maintain insight into how an endeavour is progressing—especially the behavioural metrics. Continual monitoring of the Net Engagement Score™ is particularly valuable because it provides an at-a-glance assessment of overall progress and an early indication if motivation levels are falling.

But, the aim isn't to monitor engagement so that action can be taken only when motivation waivers. Rather, engagement should be monitored so that the influence of ongoing motivational activities is better understood. The intention is continual *motivation maintenance* rather than occasional *motivation intervention*. This is important in any team activity, but especially important in collaborative endeavours, where the participants often come from a variety of backgrounds and are typically not 100 percent devoted to the endeavour. If at any point they become disillusioned, they will de-prioritise collaborative commitments and shift focus to their other responsibilities. And, if this happens, the success of the endeavour is very much in jeopardy.

Unfortunately, motivation maintenance is difficult; it requires a delicate balance of encouragement, persuasion, cajoling, and occasionally pleading. There is a huge amount of debate and discussion on the topic, and a plethora of professional psychologists—and nonprofessional management gurus—have built theories around it. But, no single theory covers all aspects of group motivation, and no single approach guarantees that all participants will be always on board and contributing to the best of their ability. As the old saying goes, it's impossible to please "*all of the people all of the time*". But, the usual fallback option of pleasing "*some of the people some of the time*" isn't good enough in a collaborative community.

The goal has to be pleasing "*almost all of the people, almost all of the time*".

So, this isn't about creating an environment where only the elite performers are happy. Rather, it's about creating an environment where *all* participants are happy and fully vested in the success of the endeavour—or at least most of them are. And this means establishing seven key conditions.

High-Motivation Environment Conditions

Sense of Direction
Information
Appropriate Resources
Minimal Distractions
Delivery on Commitments
Opportunities for Growth
Recognition

The first is something that should be present in all collaborative endeavours regardless: **a strong sense of direction**. If a good statement of purpose has been developed it will satisfy this requirement and provide a unifying element that is common to every participant. They may have different backgrounds, interests, approaches, ideas and roles to play, but all participants should have the same target outcome in mind. Even participants providing only a small contribution should feel that their involvement is part of the greater whole and without which the outcome is not assured.

There are two nuances to consider with respect to establishing a strong sense of direction. First, although flexibility in adapting goals, approaches, tasks and activities to internal and external dynamics is acceptable, the ultimate purpose of the endeavour should always remain constant. If it changes, then there is a strong chance that at least some participants will lose alignment and drop out of the community. Second, the purpose should be continually reinforced across the entire endeavour. This is why rallying cries and slogans, like Komatsu's "*Encircle Caterpillar*" are so powerful—distilling the core essence of the statement of purpose into something succinct and memorable that can be repeatedly communicated throughout the community.

The second basic condition to establish is to **keep people informed.** If participants don't feel that they are being being kept in the loop, they quickly become disenchanted and disconnected from the endeavour.[40] Conversely, when they feel that they understand what's going on and are actively involved, they are much more likely to feel fully engaged. The more open the communication channels, the less chance there is of confusion and misalignment creeping in.

This isn't only about one-way, top-down communication, it's also about cultivating bottom-up and two-way dialogue—with senior participants listening and responding to ideas, comments, questions and concerns from more junior (or less experienced) participants. It's also about nurturing communication channels that run across and through the community, so that people talk to each other as peers. In general, the more information available within the community, the greater the sense of involvement.

Of course, there will be some endeavours where a compartmentalisation of information will be necessary for security, privacy or legal reasons. But, even in those situations, participants should be kept informed with whatever information *is* appropriate to share—and, they should always be kept aware of overall progress towards the target outcome of the endeavour and how their specific responsibilities and achievements are individually contributing.[41]

The third condition to establish in a high-motivation environment is to support participants with **access to appropriate resources**. This means ensuring that they have at their disposal the core tools to fulfil their responsibilities efficiently and effectively. Although this doesn't necessarily increase motivation, it does maintain it. And the converse is certainly true; when people are forced to work with sub-standard or inappropriate tools, motivation invariably and inevitably falls.

And, it's worth noting that the provision of resources that participants wouldn't otherwise have access to—either because the endeavour is particularly well-funded or it has unique access—can have a very positive impact on motivation. The opportunity to work with interesting new tools and resources can be one of the key reasons that people join an endeavour, and this facet can be extended to any endeavour, regardless of budget, simply by embracing innovative processes. If the endeavour takes advantage of the latest

techniques and provides the opportunity for participants to
learn about or apply them, this is something that naturally
increases motivation; the availability of interesting tools,
processes and techniques directly correlates with high
community interest.

The fourth condition is to **eliminate roadblocks
and distractions**. It's a certainty that setbacks will occur
during an endeavour and nothing ever goes exactly according
to plan.[42] Unforeseen issues arise and even minor problems
are an irritation and a motivation drain. In fact,
counterintuitively, minor issues can often have a bigger impact
than more serious issues, because they get less collective
attention and the people associated with them are expected to
just go ahead and fix them themselves. This can be draining
and demotivating, especially if those minor issues are a
constant recurring theme. But, few things impress people
more than the quick removal of roadblocks and distractions;
when participants know that issues will be dealt with quickly
and effectively, their sense of engagement is reinforced and
elevated.

The process of roadblock removal encompasses three
steps. The first is to recognise that there is a problem—yet
another reason why constant evaluation is so important.
When good evaluation and communication protocols are in
place, issues are identified early and can be dealt with quickly.
If issues go unnoticed, especially if participants are just quietly
(but unhappily) dealing with them, motivation will be slowly
but surely eroded.

The second step is to review the roadblock, taking the
time to understand its size and shape—including what is
causing it and what approaches might be adopted to reduce or
eliminate it. For larger problems, this is typically a group
activity and multiple participants should be involved to analyse
the issue and find a solution. For smaller issues, a smaller team
can be assembled. But, if the same small issue continually
reappears, then it isn't enough to just fix it and move on: more
time must be invested, more people must be involved, and the
root cause must be identified and tackled.

The third and final step is to remove—or as a
minimum, reduce—the roadblock. The most important
consideration here is to understand that resolution is not the
exclusive responsibility of the owner of the relevant goal or the
orchestrator of an endeavour. In world-class endeavours,

collaboration orchestrators may be the central point for resolution, but they should strive to bring to bear all possible people, influence, and resources to deal with issues as rapidly as possible.

The fifth key condition to embed within a collaborative endeavour is the intent to always **deliver on commitments**. The most obvious manifestation of this is to ensure that the approaches, tasks and activities that comprise goals are achieved in line with expectations. This ensures that everybody within a community knows that deliverables will be completed on time, on budget, and at the appropriate level of quality and functionality. It's worth noting that this is important across an entire endeavour at all levels. Obviously, completing a core deliverable, especially one on a critical path with multiple dependencies, is a fundamental obligation. But, even small seemingly insignificant commitments can impact motivation, sometimes in a surprisingly significant way. For example, consistently starting and ending meetings on time, making personal calls when expected, and regularly distributing status updates, all build trust and promote a group ethos in which promises are expected to be kept.

Obviously, it won't always be possible to meet every commitment every time: there will be occasional unexpected and unavoidable issues. However, if the environment is one in which people generally trust one another to deliver, an occasional slip will be acceptable. This is especially true if the reason for failure is clearly understood and remediation or backup plans are rapidly implemented. Consistently missing commitments erodes confidence and lowers motivation, but consistently meeting commitments, even in the face of occasional setbacks, builds confidence and creates an atmosphere in which occasional failures are acceptable and viewed as something to overcome together.

The sixth condition is to **create opportunities for growth**. The fundamental difference between a collaborative endeavour and a solitary one is the concept of group responsibility: participants sacrifice individual return for a collective benefit, usually directly tied to the success of the endeavour. But, often another key benefit—although admittedly tangential—is the chance to participate in the endeavour and learn from those associated with it. For most participants, achieving the target outcome is the most critical consideration, but the journey to achieving the outcome and the experience gathered along the way is also important. For some, the journey is *more* important than the destination, and this is why providing opportunities for growth within the endeavour is such a significant contributor to motivation.

The good news is that collaborative endeavours often represent unique opportunities for people from different backgrounds and with different levels (and types) of experience to come together, learn from one another, and expand their experience. As such, there are several ways that they can be used as opportunities for growth.

Cultivating exposure to new ideas and new ways of doing things is the easiest method because it usually happens organically anyway—as a natural fallout of groups of people coming together to achieve something of collective interest. As endeavours progress, new ideas emerge and new processes are developed. Most of these will be directly related to the endeavour itself, helping to propel it forward, but they will often be equally relevant elsewhere and represent 'spin-off' concepts that can be explored and exploited outside. Whatever the immediate relevance, exposure to interesting and potentially valuable ideas and processes is a strong motivator that ensures that participants retain interest and enthusiasm.

Providing a platform for participants to present their own ideas is another way to introduce growth opportunities. Sometimes this is nothing more than allowing people to voice their opinions; when they feel heard, motivation and engagement increases. But, collaborative endeavours also allow for a bigger stage, where participants can present entirely new ideas that push traditional boundaries. In this case, participants can truly stretch their thinking, test out new concepts, and get support in moving them from theory to reality.

Empowering individuals to develop and apply leadership skills is a third method of providing opportunities for growth. This is about taking advantage of a useful feature of many endeavours—the potential for distributed leadership, where although there may be a central orchestrator, different people can take responsibility for leading different elements or phases of the endeavour. This can be particularly interesting for junior participants who may not have leadership opportunities in their day-to-day roles. By assuming greater authority within the collaborative endeavour, they can gain experience and showcase their managerial prowess. Seasoned participants can also find motivation in exercising leadership skills, but their sense of fulfilment will come from having their expertise recognised and valued rather than from cultivating new abilities.

A final method of creating opportunities for growth is to nurture or create cross-pollination, allowing participants to move around within the community and build experience and contacts. This is often a very attractive feature since it provides participants with the chance to move beyond day-to-day areas of responsibility, network with other people, and perhaps find exciting new roles. It's more difficult than the other three methods mentioned, since it isn't a natural outgrowth of group dynamics, but it is possible in almost all endeavours. The trick is to find ways for participants to be exposed to different people, different approaches, and different working environments[43]—all valued and valuable experiences.

The seventh and final condition for high motivation is to **acknowledge performance and effort.** At its most basic, this is nothing more elaborate than recognising participant contribution. People like to feel that their effort is noticed, and even small messages of appreciation are highly valued; an occasional note or comment can go a long way. At a slightly higher level, broader recognition within the collaborative community is more powerful because it builds peer respect. And, public praise has a unique property in that it motivates not only those who receive it, but also those around them, who strive to achieve the same level of recognition. This is especially true when the recognition is based on above and beyond performance or overcoming challenges to achieve something that has a positive impact on the larger group.

Acknowledgement of effort doesn't have to be only for success and although it isn't common, there is room for recognising occasional missteps too. Outstanding effort that didn't generate positive results—occasionally even outright failure—can still be lauded if it made an important contribution to the endeavour as a whole. This is especially true in highly ambitious endeavours where boundaries are being pushed and occasional failure has to be accepted as a constant possibility. Setbacks that build knowledge and understanding should be recognised and rewarded, not swept aside and forgotten.

In terms of rewards, tangible incentives like money and gifts have their place, but it's the intangible rewards that often have the greatest impact. For example, in the military, physically low-value items (like medals) can hold immense emotional value. The armed forces assemble people in miserable conditions and still motivate them to the level where they are willing to die for an endeavour. However you look at it, that's true motivation and there's a lot to be learned from it. In fact, periods of adversity and challenge are often the environments in which motivation rises and community camaraderie is deeply reinforced.

It's important to note that acknowledging performance isn't only about good performance: it's equally important to address poor performance. This is most obvious when milestones are missed and deliverables are not delivered on time and on budget. But, there are other less obvious forms of underperformance too, such as failure to meet acceptable standards, non-compliance with agreed policies, or just general, but subtle, dissent.[44] These can be every bit as insidious as missed deliverables, but rather than creating immediate drops in motivation they manifest as a slow but steady erosion of morale.

No matter what form it takes, underperformance is a serious problem and must be addressed. Of course, the reaction can't simply be the automatic removal or replacement of an individual or team; if this is done without some attempt to understand the underlying issues it would not only be unfair, but also futile and demotivating to other participants. Instead, it's important to ensure that the basics for success have been covered.

First, check that success is a genuine possibility. If an individual or team has been assigned a responsibility that is beyond any realistic expectation of success, nobody will be able to complete it. In such an instance the issue isn't underperformance at all, it's an overestimation of general attainability. Next, check that the appropriate tools to do the job have been provided; if the tools are absent, it's unreasonable to expect that it will be completed. Third, check

---

Underperformance Considerations

Achievable Goals
Relevant Tools
Suitable Environment
Appropriate Capabilities

that the operating environment is appropriate because expecting people to be successful in a hostile environment is both unreasonable and impractical. Finally, check that the person or people assigned the responsibility have the capabilities to achieve it.

If any of these considerations are sub-optimal, the problem isn't actually underperformance at all, but unrealistic support and expectations, and these must be fixed as quickly as possible to bring the endeavour back on track. Only then, if performance is still deemed to be a problem, is it time to look elsewhere for delivery of the assigned responsibilities.

CASE STUDY
***Maiden* in the Whitbread Round The World Yacht Race**

The Ocean Race is one of the most difficult and challenging competitive events on the planet. Originally called the Whitbread Round the World Race after its founding sponsor, it pits sailing crews against each other, and the elements, as they circumnavigate the globe in a series of gruelling stages that push humans and boats to the very limits of endurance.

For the 1985/86 race, one of the competitors was twenty-three year old Tracy Edwards—one of only four women out of a total of 260 crew positions across fifteen boats. The race was a defining moment in Edwards' life, and despite the immense challenges and deprivations that she experienced during the race, she had caught the bug. She now desperately wanted to compete again, but next time in a more senior role. Unfortunately, she knew that the heavily male-dominated world of open ocean sailing would never provide her with that opportunity and the best that she could hope for was another junior crew position.

Unless of course … she entered her own boat.

What followed were three years of incredible effort, overcoming obstacles that would have easily defeated most people. Sponsors were queuing up to pour millions into custom-designed boats, crewed by famous male yachtsmen, but nobody was willing to invest anything in Edwards' vision. Undeterred, she followed her dream anyway, and in 1987 took the first essential step: mortgaging her house to buy *Prestige*, a beautiful yacht built in 1979 that had fallen into serious disrepair. Edwards enlisted a team of women and together they entirely rebuilt *Prestige*, renamed her *Maiden*, then sailed her in the 1988 Route of Discovery Race from Cadiz to Santa Domingo—which they won.

Unfortunately, even with this win under her belt, Edwards still struggled to reach the starting line for the 1989/90 round the world race. Money was an ever-present challenge and the intensely misogynistic yachting media poured ridicule on her endeavour, making it supremely difficult to secure sponsorship and financial support.

Despite all of her effort, her dream was fading, until she got support from an unexpected quarter—King Hussein of Jordan. Edwards had met the king a few years earlier when she was a crew member on a short cruise with him. They had hit it off, remained in touch, and he now stepped up to encourage and support her. Most importantly, he brought Royal Jordanian Airlines as *Maiden's* primary sponsor.

So, against all odds, *Maiden* left Southampton on 2 September and lined up in The Solent with twenty-three other yachts for the start of the race.

The first leg, to Punta del Este in Uruguay, proved to be a challenging but unifying experience. The crew melded as a team and skills soared with experience. They began to understand the boat and each other. But, with calm weather plaguing much of the leg, they didn't get the opportunity to fully demonstrate their prowess and finished third in their class. Still, it was a creditable performance and the previously dismissive sailing community suddenly began to pay attention.

Leg 2, from Punta del Este to Fremantle, started on 28 September—and this was when *Maiden* came into her own. Edwards' expertise as a navigator came to the fore when she plotted a course to move steadily southwards, taking advantage of developing weather systems. Six days in, sailing in strong winds and mountainous seas dotted with lethal icebergs, her course proved to be the right choice and *Maiden* took the lead.

Over the next thirty days, Edwards continued to navigate skilfully. Despite failures of both the satellite navigation and weather reporting systems, the crew came together as a unit, dealing with everything that the Southern Ocean could throw at them. Competitor boats pushed them hard, but Edwards continued to make the right decisions and the crew continued to translate those decisions into top-performance sailing. On 3 December, they sailed into

Fremantle at the end of the 7,260 nautical mile leg as the first boat in their class and the best ever finish for a British boat in the Whitbread Round the World Yacht Race.

World-class sailing expertise was what propelled *Maiden* to Fremantle, but it was a determination to succeed that brought ultimate victory. Edwards not only skilfully navigated *Maiden* across the Southern Ocean, she equally skilfully created an environment in which the crew were fully committed to performing at the very best of their capabilities: putting everything in place to create an environment of unprecedented high motivation.

- She provided a powerful sense of direction. Not only were the crew a team of true competitors with a determination to win, they were also a group of women fuelled by a desire to show the sailing community—and especially the sailing media—that female sailors are every bit as good as their male counterparts.
- She kept the crew fully briefed about all aspects of the race at all times. She was the navigator and skipper of the boat, and it was her sole responsibility to decide what course to take, but she kept everybody informed about her decision-making process and the associated consequences. She willingly explained her rationale, and twice a day plotted the positions of all of the other boats in the race so that everybody could see how they were performing.
- She ensured that the crew had all of the tools and resources necessary to compete effectively. The conditions were far from ideal—they never would be on a 18 m yacht in the middle of the unforgiving Southern Ocean—but the crew had everything that they needed for success. More importantly, when they had the occasional but inevitable failures that plague any high-risk endeavour—which for *Maiden* included problematic computers, malfunctioning satellite navigation systems, unreliable weather reports, defective water purification technology, poor quality fuel and faulty compasses—Edwards took them in her stride and effectively worked around them until fixes were made.
- Edwards used the first leg of the race to develop the crew, building expertise and allowing them to grow as both individuals and team members. There were occasional mistakes, but she ensured that these were seen as learning opportunities so that, when they entered the Southern

Ocean, the team was battle-hardened and ready for the challenges that were thrown at them. When individuals performed well, there was praise and recognition. When there were occasional errors of judgement or ability, there was coaching and guidance.

Maiden went on to win the second leg of the race, from Uruguay to Fremantle, and the third leg from Fremantle to Auckland, but on the fourth leg a serious leak developed and slowed the boat considerably—bad enough that at some periods there was genuine concern that she might sink! Then, on the fifth leg, bad luck led to *Maiden* sailing in suboptimal conditions that lost them yet more time. In the end, she finished the race second in her class, behind the much better funded *L'Esprit de Liberté*.

It was a fantastic achievement and Edwards, *Maiden* and her all-female crew[45] had redefined ocean racing forever, proving that female sailors aren't just as good as their male counterparts, they are very often better.

In 1990, Tracy Edwards was deservedly named Yachtsman of the Year: the first woman to receive that enviable accolade.

Motivation is a multi-faceted aspect of collaborative endeavours. It binds participants together and drives them through the stages of group development that are rarely—some might say never—smooth. Building and maintaining it is not just about intervention when motivation slips, but about proactively sustaining it throughout the lifetime of an endeavour. Ultimately, the challenge is to create an environment where all participants feel motivated and directly connected to the endeavour's success, thereby maximising collective performance and achieving shared goals.

There is one final point that should be understood when structuring a collaborative environment for maximum possible motivation: although it may seem counterintuitive, some participants will contribute most effectively when operating in isolation. This is a characteristic of group dynamics that is often overlooked, and businesses in particular are often guilty of placing an over-emphasis on teamwork where people work together. But, there are some individuals who prefer to work in teams, independently. This preference doesn't signify disengagement from the community or a lack of commitment to achieving collective goals; rather, it reflects an inclination towards solitary work. It's essential to acknowledge and accommodate these preferences when establishing conditions for collaborative endeavours, especially if these individuals have key capabilities crucial to overall success.

The Apollo Program

The Apollo program took place in a very different era. The 1960s were an inflection point in US society as the nation experienced an economic boom notable for its duration and breadth and defined by a massive growth in employment, significant reductions in taxes, and a globally enviable increase in GDP. There were certainly issues —Vietnam, the Cuban missile crisis, inflation and the emergence of a rebellious

Katherine Johnson - Image courtesy: NASA

new youth counter-culture—but, in general the entire nation had a sense of positive expectation for the future.

There was one group in particular for whom the 1960s represented a defining era: African Americans. The decade started with the Freedom Riders—a group of black and white activists who rode buses together to test the boundaries of a 1960 Supreme Court decision that declared the segregation of interstate transportation facilities as unconstitutional. It went on to witness the 1963 'March on Washington', the 1964 Civil Rights Act, and the 1965 Voting Rights Act. While there were terrible events such as the assassination of Martin Luther King and the "Bloody Sunday" violence at Montgomery, Alabama, the decade was a period of unprecedented progress towards racial equality.

One of those who took advantage of the social advances of the period was Katherine Johnson, a gifted mathematician from White Sulphur Springs in West Virginia. As a girl, she skipped multiple grades and was pushed to high school at just 10 years of age, four years ahead of her classmates. This was an impressive achievement for any child, but a truly incredible accomplishment for an African American girl. She went on to graduate high school at 14 and college at 18, before going on to be a school teacher. She then married, had children and settled down into what looked set to be a typical life for a woman of the time.

But, at age 35, everything changed. She was recruited by the National Advisory Committee for Aeronautics (NACA) who were employing women as 'computers' for the tedious and precise work of measuring and calculating wind tunnel tests. She joined an all-female African American team at the Langley Research Center's Guidance and Navigation Department and then, when NASA subsumed NACA, Katherine found herself working on the Apollo program.

Her reputation at NASA grew rapidly and she was viewed as one of its most accomplished computers. She was personally responsible for manually calculating the trajectory for Alan Shepard's 'Freedom 7' space flight, and even when NASA started to use electronic computers she was used to check that the machines had got it right. John Glenn personally requested that Katherine recheck the calculations for his Friendship 7 flight and she went on to play a critical role throughout the Apollo program—including with the Apollo 11 mission—and beyond, right up to the launch of the space shuttle.

At first glance, it might seem that the environment at NASA would not be conducive to Katherine and the countless other women who worked there. They faced undeniable racial and sexual discrimination; they were segregated, worked in conditions that were more challenging than those of their white male colleagues, and were denied senior management positions. And yet, despite these barriers, they were still highly motivated. Some of this is down to the era in which they lived, when people such as Katherine just accepted the conditions under which they worked. But, it was more than that; a lot of the core components of motivation were present at NASA.

Katherine, and the other computers, had an exceptionally strong sense of direction and were kept informed of project dynamics at all times. They knew that their work was instrumental to the success of the Apollo program, represented a critical component, and intersected with the work of other groups within the organisation. They had access to the resources necessary to do their jobs and they got the chance to use truly cutting-edge tools as NASA brought in emerging technology from organisations such as IBM, MIT and AT&T. Their working environment was at times challenging, but NASA worked hard to deliver on commitments and eliminate roadblocks. They were recognised, acknowledged and rewarded for their effort and had career opportunities that were unavailable anywhere else in the United States.

Despite the barriers of a white male-dominated environment, Katherine and her colleagues had all of the core components that support a high-performance environment. To their credit, NASA worked hard to augment their inherent strength of character to ensure that, despite very real challenges to their morale, they never wavered in their determination and motivation to succeed.

Mediate

$$\frac{dH}{dt} = f(A,N,C)$$

All collaborative endeavours will, at some point, suffer from disharmony, and even simple endeavours will encounter occasional problems. The loftier the ambition, the more numerous the participants, and the more complex the approaches, tasks and activities, the greater the chance of conflict arising.

It's true that a well-designed endeavour is less likely to suffer conflict. For example, a carefully crafted statement of purpose will reduce the chances of misalignments of vision and frequent updates to a lexicon will minimise communication misunderstandings. But, it is inevitable that there will be occasional friction as people make different interpretations of situations, struggle to harness high-demand resources, and cope with adverse environmental factors. Even when endeavours are progressing smoothly, accidental adversity can occur when people unintentionally 'trip over' one another despite the best intentions. When disagreements and disputes do arise, it's essential to actively manage them, balancing results and relationships to mediate[46] effective resolutions.[47]

Collaborative Mediation

Avoid
Accommodate
Confront
Compromise

The quickest and easiest way to do this is to either *avoid* the issue (wait for it to go away or resolve itself), or *accommodate* concerns (play down tensions and sooth bruised egos). On the surface, this may seem like a naive, short-sighted or even negligent approach. After all, disagreements rarely improve with age, and placating hurt feelings doesn't usually materially change anything. Sweeping conflict under the carpet usually means that it will simply need to be addressed at some point in the future—by which time it may have developed into something much more difficult to deal with. But, there is room for adopting these approaches when dealing with issues of relatively low importance, and in the following three specific circumstances: first, if the source of conflict is something that is expected to change for the better in the near future; second, if the conflict is genuinely irresolvable because of rigid constraints such as time, money or resources; and third, if the conflict is based on superficial differences of opinion or personality where it's possible to agree to disagree.

Of course, when issues are of higher importance and critical collaborator relationships could be damaged, more active conflict management techniques are necessary—such as *confrontation* and *compromise*. These are more difficult, and can at times be uncomfortable, but will almost always produce better long-term results.

As techniques, they exist on a spectrum, with confrontation at one end and compromise at the other. Confrontation is most appropriate when quick, decisive action is needed or when resolution options are likely to be somewhat unpopular with all parties. In such instances, settlement should be presented as a fait accompli with debate structured only around finding the least-worst resolution. This will inevitably result in some level of dissatisfaction, but can be the best option at times, and the only option in some circumstances.

At the other end of the spectrum, compromise is based on the premise that all participants involved in the conflict are willing to sacrifice something for the greater good of the endeavour. It's the appropriate option when conflicts are many-sided and complex, but it still requires a general willingness from all parties to work together to look for common ground. It's a more equitable and conciliatory approach—where participants may not be completely happy with a specific resolution, but at least feel that it is reasonable and that they have been treated fairly.

Interestingly, this sense of being fairly treated and resolving issues can elevate conflict resolution to the point that it isn't a negative-oriented activity. In fact, when done effectively it can have a markedly positive impact on a collaborative community. It adds time and complexity to day-to-day progress, but it also drives dialogue which in turn clarifies opinions and perspectives. It can illuminate different points of view that might otherwise go unnoticed and help collaborators better understand and appreciate one another. In the best-case scenario, disagreements and misunderstandings that are skilfully addressed by active mediation can bring teams closer together and increase team cohesion.

But, to do this, an integrative approach to conflict resolution must be adopted, and that means working

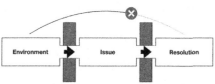

through a series of three consecutive mediation stages: creating an environment for discussion, exploring the issue(s) and finally, agreeing on a resolution. Throughout the process, the objective is to move as rapidly as possible without skipping ahead or skimming over important considerations.

The first stage of the process, **creating an environment for discussion**, involves clarifying four areas.

First, the mediator role, which is to facilitate the process and where necessary

Creating an Environment for Discussion

Clarify Roles
Embrace Compromise
Set Timeframes
Establish Ground Rules

act as arbitrator. The focus is on helping everybody speak openly and understand one another's different points of view. At all times, the mediator should be focused on achieving the target outcome of the endeavour, not on any one party to the conflict. The mediator should only take sides if an issue threatens to overwhelm the endeavour and no integrative solution can be found.

Second, acknowledge that life is rarely, if ever, perfect. Compromise is not only acceptable but desirable and it's infinitely better to share success than have no success at all. Even in confrontational situations it's almost always better to find a mutually agreeable solution than to fight a battle for supremacy. After all, the easiest—and most effective—way to overcome an enemy is by transforming them into an ally.

Third, set time limits, which should be demanding because the objective is to reach resolution as quickly as possible, but also practical and realistic because the solution has to be acceptable to all parties. It's important to instil a strong sense of urgency and to accept the need to work hard to reach resolution, but not rush people into accepting something that will be unacceptable in the long term.

And fourth, establish basic ground rules for everybody to operate by. These will be unique to every endeavour, but some generic ideas to start with are:

- **Confidentiality**: discussions should be kept within the group and not communicated more broadly without explicit agreement from all parties.
- **Flexibility and Openness**: all parties should engage on the assumption that there is an acceptable resolution.
- **Creativity**: the best solution is not to simply find an acceptable middle ground, but to find a new and better higher ground.
- **Honesty**: while it's acceptable and natural to want to keep cards close to the chest during periods of uncertainty and disharmony, mistruths or misdirections are unacceptable .[48]
- **Mutual Respect**: all participants should discuss differences in ways that allow everybody to both demonstrate and retain dignity.[49]

Once the environment has been established and agreed, the next stage of collaborative mediation is to **explore the issues(s)**. This can initially be challenging, especially for highly charged conflicts, and

> ### Exploring Issues
>
> Reiterate Purpose
> Define Issue
> Clarify Positions
> Agree Ground Rules
> Identify Points of Difference

early dialogue can become unhelpfully heated if emotions take precedence over reason. So, rather than launch straight into the problem, it's a good tactic to start the conversation by reiterating the purpose of the endeavour and ensuring agreement. It's always useful to make sure that participants remain aligned to the endeavour as a concept, and focusing initially on something that everybody should agree on provides a safe starting point for discussion.

Once general dialogue has been established, hopefully with emotions at least somewhat in check if not completely eliminated, discussion can move into more contentious territory. The best way is to do this without unnecessarily escalating tensions is by focusing on clarifying the size and shape of the issue with input from multiple perspectives. Wherever possible, this dialogue should be structured around facts rather than opinion,[50] with emphasis on defining and understanding the issue. The best technique is to avoid talking about people and personalities—unless of course they are the issue—and instead objectify it by discussing actions and effects, contributory factors, perceived constraints, and impacts and outcomes.[51]

Next, move on to positions. This is likely to be where the dialogue will become more emotive and it's almost impossible to avoid that. But, taking the time to get people talking before jumping straight into the sources of disagreement should diffuse the situation to some degree and keep the conversation reasonably well contained. However, it's important to understand that all parties will have agendas—conscious and unconscious, stated and unstated. Good mediation involves making every effort to make all parties aware of the agendas in play, and attempting to alleviate concerns around them. The priority should be to keep perspectives open and to help all parties see the situation from firstly their own perspective, then from the other party's perspective, and finally from the mediator's—neutral third-party—perspective.

To accomplish this, each side should be given the opportunity to explain, without interruption, how they see the situation and the sources of conflict and disagreement. A useful framework is for each party to explain their position from:

- Their understanding of the situation.
- How this has or is affecting them.
- Their perception of the consequences if things don't change.

People in conflict don't always listen to one another as attentively as they should, so following each stated position, it's a good idea to summarise what was said; this further reinforces statements and keeps misunderstandings to a minimum.

Once each party has had the chance to explain their position, the next step is to define the points of difference and agreement. Establishing consensus here provides clarity on what needs to be resolved while instituting a frame of reference in which resolution is possible. It's not uncommon for issues that appeared to be insurmountable at the start of a mediation to become less overwhelming once they are clearly defined. And, clarifying areas of common ground creates a sense of shared goals, values, and purpose that reduces tensions and can even build a sense of understanding and rapport.

Once all of the issues have been fully discussed, the third and final stage of the mediation process is to **identify and accept a resolution**. Note the word *accept*. In an ideal situation, and the majority of the time, a resolution will be agreed. But, there will be instances when the resolution is not agreed to by everyone and is simply … accepted. The general rule of thumb is, if everybody is eighty percent comfortable with the resolution, and no better option can be found, this should be good enough to accept it and move on.

The search for resolution is much like any other brainstorming exercise: all parties to the conflict should first brainstorm possible resolutions, then assemble them for clarification, de-duplication and consolidation, and finally prioritise and select those that are the most appropriate. This can be a lengthy process, but should never be rushed. Even

when there is a seemingly obvious resolution, with everybody
ready to accept it, it's still worth taking the time to thoroughly
explore its feasibility from all angles and look at other
alternatives.

      This is important for three reasons. First, the
majority of resolutions will involve some level of compromise,
and this must be fully understood and appreciated by all
parties for it to be successful in the long term. Second, even
when one resolution appears to be the best option, there may
be components of other resolutions that could be incorporated
within it to make it even better.[52] And third, eighty percent of
mediation sticking points appear in the last twenty percent of a
mediation, and brushing aside problems in the excitement of
reaching a conclusion can result in resolutions that fall apart
later, when everybody has departed.

CASE STUDY
Elon Musk vs Twitter

A great example of how (not) to deal with dispute and disagreement, is the Elon Musk acquisition of Twitter. It wasn't the worst-ever business deal—that's an accolade generally attributed to Bayer's 2015 acquisition of Monsanto —but it certainly ranks up there alongside AOL's merger with Time Warner and Bank of America's acquisition of Countrywide.

Musk's motivation for the Twitter purchase is unclear. His critics have suggested that it was a desire to exert control over a communication channel to which he was heavily emotionally connected and that had not shown him due deference. Musk's stated position was that he wanted to introduce a range of new features, make Twitter's algorithms transparent, combat spambot accounts, and promote global discussion and free speech. Certainly, Musk has consistently denied that it was a financially motivated endeavour, and that much is undoubtedly true since X (formerly Twitter) is currently valued at somewhere between thirty-five and forty-five percent of what Musk paid for it.

Musk had been a prolific Twitter user for many years, and an increasingly vocal critic. He clashed with the platform on several occasions and voiced frustration with its leadership. As early as 2017 he had floated the idea of making a bid for the company, but in early 2022 something clicked—and he began buying stock, building up to a majority 9.1 percent stake. Then on 14 April, he announced an acquisition bid with an offer of $54.20 per share, which valued Twitter at a staggering $44 bn. Twitter initially resisted the deal, but after two weeks changed its mind and unanimously voted to accept Musk's offer.

We can't know what was going on in Musk's mind, but he was perhaps a little surprised by the sudden Twitter capitulation, and took a more clear-headed look at the numbers. Whatever the reason, on 13 May 2022, Musk announced that the deal was on hold, citing Twitter misrepresentation of the number of spambot accounts on the platform. Twitter responded that as far as it was concerned, the deal was going ahead and would be legally enforced if necessary. A month later, Musk applied more pressure by announcing that he was withdrawing from the deal altogether, and then re-asserted his position again in July. But, Twitter appeared unfazed and this time responded with a lawsuit, with a trial scheduled for mid-October.

Twitter's aggressive stance was probably a surprise to Musk, and despite attempts to bluster his way forward—formally informing both the SEC and Twitter that he was withdrawing—he eventually backed down a few weeks before the trial was due to start and announced that the deal was going ahead; it closed on 27 October.

Independent statistics show that X—the new Musk company that was formerly Twitter—was the 12th most popular social media platform in 2024 with significant declines in traffic, active users, app downloads and, most important of all, advertising revenue. By almost any measure, the acquisition is considered a failed endeavour and this can be largely attributed to a conflict resolution approach that was flawed from the start. Instead of creating a positive environment for discussion and debate, it was deeply adversarial with no apparent desire to reach any kind of mutually beneficial solution. Confrontation was the general strategy and neither Musk nor Twitter demonstrated any flexibility, creativity or mutual respect.

Early in the dispute, there were opportunities for something positive to come out of the situation. Indeed, when Twitter offered Musk a seat on the board of directors—a position where he could have had a strong influence over the company and its future direction—CEO Parag Agrawal wrote that he believed Musk's appointment would bring long-term value to the company. Twitter co-founder and former CEO Jack Dorsey wrote that Musk "*cares deeply about our world and Twitter's role in it*". Even after Musk stepped back from the board less than a week later, Agrawal stated that Twitter would "*remain open to his input*". But arrogance, over-inflated egos and personal animosity got in the way of finding any kind of common ground and instead of exploring issues, clarifying positions and striving for an integrative solution, the Musk and Twitter teams withdrew from dialogue and accelerated to legal proceedings.

It's possible that X could recover and reassert itself as a relevant social media platform—after all, it is still the pre-eminent channel for news distribution globally. But, it will require a lot of work including a much-needed injection of strong leadership. At this point, X's most powerful characteristic is as an excellent case study of how to actively avoid productive discussion, negotiate badly, and pay an unnecessarily premium price.

The Musk/Twitter example is almost exactly the opposite of how mediation should be approached. The objective should be to reach an acceptable resolution as quickly as possible and with the minimum possible impact on the community. It isn't always possible, and there are times when no universally acceptable resolution will be found—there may even be times when no resolution at all can be found and the outcome of the mediation will be the less than ideal action of accepting one party's position over another—but, in most instances, mediation *will* result in a resolution and an endeavour will find a way forward.

What really makes the difference is the skill, experience and ingenuity of the mediator. Mediation is a role that is certainly easier for people who have an inherent ability for conflict resolution, but it's also something that can be learned—and practice dramatically improves skills. Good mediators tend to demonstrate core expertise in taking control of situations, acting as both spokespeople and facilitators, and actively striving to appreciate arguments from all sides. They are particularly adept at managing three critical areas. First, influence and power, because the side that has the most power has a key advantage. Second, information and understanding, because the side that has the most knowledge has a key advantage. And third, time and flexibility, because the side with the most time has a key advantage. A good mediator works hard to level the playing field in these three areas, thereby minimising power bases and driving everybody towards resolution rather than victory.

The Apollo Program

Throughout the 1960s, NASA was constantly pushing the boundaries of science and technology, and the stakes were quite literally, life or death. In such an environment it's hardly surprising that there were occasional misunderstandings and

John Houbolt - Image courtesy: NASA

differences of opinion based on strongly held perspectives and preconceptions. And, it's equally unsurprising that those misunderstandings and differences led to internal conflict. In fact, it would have been incredible if that had not been the case.

One of the biggest conflicts associated with the Apollo program occurred very early in the initiative, with fundamentally different views across the organisation regarding what 'mission mode' should be adopted. Four primary options were under consideration:

- **Direct-Ascent (DA)**: where a single spacecraft would be launched as a complete unit which would then travel to the Moon, land on it, and return to Earth.
- **Earth-Orbit Rendezvous (EOR)**: where multiple launches (up to 15 in some plans) would send various components into Earth orbit for assembly into a single spacecraft that would then travel to the Moon and back.
- **Lunar-Surface Rendezvous (LSR)**: where two spacecraft would be launched in succession. The first would be a non-crewed (automated) mission carrying supplies (most importantly fuel). The second would be a crewed mission which, after landing on the Moon, would be refuelled and replenished from the first for the return journey back to Earth.
- **Lunar-Orbit Rendezvous (LOR)**: where a modular spacecraft would be launched to the Moon. Upon arrival, one of the modules would remain in orbit while the other would detach and travel to the lunar surface. Following lunar exploration, the Lunar Module would then return to,

and reconnect with, the orbiting module before a return
journey to Earth.

Although all four options had pros and cons, direct-
ascent was the one initially favoured by most of NASA,
primarily because of a strong desire to avoid the complexity of
rendezvous and docking manoeuvres in space. But, there was
a small minority that felt that lunar-orbit rendezvous was the
better option. They argued that while direct-ascent was
certainly possible, the fundamental physics required to launch
such a huge spacecraft would be tremendously difficult and
prohibitively expensive. Similarly, they argued that the Earth-
orbit rendezvous option would be costly and complicated from
a design and deployment perspective, and landing a large
spacecraft on the Moon would be similarly difficult. Lunar-
orbit rendezvous was not without immense challenges, but
those who supported it had a vision of how those challenges
could be overcome.

One particularly vocal advocate for lunar-orbit
rendezvous was John Houbolt of the Langley Research Center.
He presented it as the only viable option to a series of
committees and research groups. He also mentioned it to
Robert Seamans, the NASA Associate Administrator, when he
visited Langley in 1960, and was subsequently invited to
Washington to present it to a broader group. But, he was
disappointed to find that when he got there, Seamans wasn't
part of the meeting. His ideas were met with strong opposition
and one engineer even suggested that Houbolt's carefully
drafted figures were incorrect.

Annoyed and aggrieved, Houbolt returned home and
then bypassed organisational hierarchy by sending a letter
direct to Seamans outlining his arguments. He received a
polite reply, but it was still a "no", with Seamans pointing out
that multiple committees had concluded that lunar-orbit
rendezvous was the least attractive of the options under
consideration. Undeterred, Houbolt responded with a second
letter—nine pages of single-spaced text—that began with the
statement "Somewhat as a voice in the wilderness, I would like
to pass on a few thoughts on matters that have been of deep
concern to me". To his credit, Seamans didn't just ignore the
letter; he read it, thought about it, and passed it to others for
analysis and comment. He also started to appreciate that the
level of division within the organisation over a key program

consideration was becoming more than just a minor disagreement and was beginning to threaten the success of the entire endeavour. He recognised that some level of mediation was necessary.

Seamans authorised a task force headed by his special technical assistant, Nicholas E. Golovin, and solicited opinion from across the Agency. Broader discussion and debate was encouraged, and every effort was made to switch from people defending their favourite mission mode to people exploring the details of every possible mode. This was a key turning point, especially when issues with the direct-ascent and Earth-orbit rendezvous options began to emerge, and the ability of these options to meet end-of-decade deadlines looked increasingly unlikely.

Finally, after weeks of dialogue and investigation, the committee recommended in favour of a hybrid Earth-orbit/lunar-orbit rendezvous mission mode, and the different divisions of NASA coalesced. The selection of the mission mode was officially announced in June 1962, and from then on, became the focus of everything that was to come thereafter.

The story of the selection of the Apollo mission mode is a testament to the importance of mediated dialogue in both formal and informal settings. If Houbolt hadn't persistently advocated his position, Seamans hadn't recognised the growing threat of program paralysis, Golovin hadn't skilfully orchestrated a task force, and a slew of other key individuals hadn't made the effort to work together behind the scenes, there could have been a very different outcome. It's possible, but by no means assured, that the United States would still have put a man on the Moon and returned him safely back to Earth. But, it's highly unlikely that this would have happened by 31 December 1969.

As a postscript, by the time Apollo 11 journeyed to the Moon, Houbolt had left NASA, but he was invited to Mission Control as a guest. When the lander touched down at Mare Tranquillitatis, Wernher von Braun is captured on film turning to Houbolt and saying, "*Thank you, John*".

Innovate

> ### *Tsunamis are impressive, but rare, hard to predict and very difficult to ride*

Innovation is one of those things that is highly revered, especially in business circles. The ability to innovate, and then transform, is viewed as a key differentiator for any organisation, and new market entrants equipped with pioneering innovations can move from unknown, to challenger, to leader almost overnight.

The fact is, the actions that drive success today may not have the same effect in the future, and if you don't continue to think of a better way of doing things, somebody else probably will.

Certainly, the big consulting firms regularly publish case studies that describe how businesses that "*successfully harness the power of innovation*" are twice as profitable as those that don't. Of course, these consulting firms are hardly impartial since they all have lucrative transformation practices and are keen to promote the importance of innovation programmes. But, there is a solid majority view that organisations that embrace innovation have a significant competitive advantage over their peers. They define the rules, rather than having them defined for them.

And yet, many companies that establish innovation and transformation initiatives, often with the assistance of highly paid consultants, see low impact and minimal return on investment. Interesting, market-exploitable ideas remain elusive, and a promised exciting new culture of innovation doesn't emerge as strongly as was hoped. Instead, the initiatives burn through budget and distract the organisation from its core competencies—sometimes doing more harm than good.

This lack of success can be attributed to a variety of factors, but one of the most common is a chronic and rudimentary misconception about what innovation is. This then leads to a misalignment of strategic focus on *fundamental innovation*—big, groundbreaking ideas that are the basis of tsunami transformation that requires huge leaps forward. Emphasis is focused on change that is revolutionary in scope and based on entirely new ways of doing things.

The problem is, programmes that focus primarily—or extensively—on fundamental innovation are enormously expensive. They need big budgets because uncovering large-scale, high-impact ideas is supremely difficult.[53] And, to make matters worse, even when deep funding pools are available, fundamental innovation often doesn't originate from structured transformation initiatives. Instead, it often comes from unstructured tangential activities such as those in operational groups where people have sudden flashes of brilliance, or in small teams that stumble on interesting by-products while working on something totally unrelated.

And, even when fundamental transformation initiatives *do* uncover potentially lucrative breakthrough ideas, their size and scope make them tremendously difficult to capitalise on. To do so is disruptive, distracting and disconcerting for any organisation; it introduces conflict and internal adversity that can impede as much as expedite, as people struggle to adjust to new ways of thinking that don't always appear to be an improvement on the old ways. There is usually a small minority of people who like to push boundaries and genuinely operate 'outside of the box', but most people don't; even when new ways of thinking are clearly and recognisably better, most people still don't adapt well to change.

Executives and senior leaders are particularly clumsy at embracing innovation, despite what they like to think. They put it near the top of their list of strategic priorities and launch comprehensive transformation initiatives, but a strong risk aversion reinforced over many years means that they usually fail to actively promote anything particularly new or interesting —even when it is placed directly in front of them. Most executives much prefer to stay with what they know and trust, especially when things appear to be working just fine. Given the choice, they will almost always choose the path that created historical success, and will rarely take to heart the controversial philosophy of *"if it ain't broke, break it"*.[54]

And, ninety percent of the time, they're correct! Focusing on tried-and-tested methods is typically the fastest and most effective way of moving from A to B. The truth is, that while fundamental innovation has the acknowledged potential to generate stratospheric benefits, it is expensive, unusual, and notoriously difficult to execute.

But, there is another type of innovation that is less expensive and much less disruptive: instead of being revolutionary, *incremental innovation* is evolutionary.

- It creates small but meaningful change based on ideas and approaches that can be adopted quickly and easily. Instead of requiring people to cope with huge transformation tsunamis, incremental innovation is about riding smaller transformation waves[55] leading to cumulative impact.
- It can be more easily monitored, and as new ideas emerge they can be evaluated and adjusted as necessary. Those that show promise can be refined and brought to full-scale development, while those that don't can be temporarily or permanently deprioritised.
- It provides a modest but solid foundation for that elusive culture of innovation because the periodic adoption of new ideas helps people become accustomed to change. Somewhat ironically, a by-product of frequent incremental innovation is an increased capacity to accept and cope with occasional fundamental innovation.

CASE STUDY **The Redefinition of** **Technology Services**	A great example of incremental innovation is the story of Electronic Data Systems (EDS), the company

that redefined how business technology is purchased, owned and utilised.

In 1962, *IT services* was already an established business model. IBM, the undisputed king of computer systems, had a Service Bureau division with 20,000 employees and a Datacenter business unit that provided access to mainframe computers for organisations that couldn't afford to buy their own. But, it viewed services as a means to an end: treating it as a channel for hardware sales rather than as a revenue stream in its own right. For example, when a customer signed a Datacenter deal, it was to access computer processing time by the hour, nothing more. The customers themselves had to determine how to use that time. So, IBM Datacenter was really IBM selling its own hardware to itself, and then offsetting the sale by charging out processing time to customers; a brilliant strategy for any hardware-oriented company.[56]

But Ross Perot, a highly successful salesperson at IBM, realised that his employer's perspective was limited and IT services could be much more. So, when he was given the opportunity to take on a part-time management position at Blue Cross of Texas, he jumped. His new role allowed him to split his time between his new employer and establishing his own business based on an incremental innovation over IBM's services philosophy.

His concept was simple: there were lots of organisations that *underutilised* the very expensive IBM equipment that they owned, and other organisations that wanted access to more; if those organisations could be brought together, symbiotic relationships could be brokered whereby the underutilised processing time at one organisation could be exploited by another.

He tested his concept on James Ralph Woods, the Chairman of Southwestern Life—an insurance company to whom he had sold an IBM 7070 mainframe computer two years previously. He knew that Southwestern was running that computer eight hours a day, but it sat idle for the remaining sixteen; that was sixteen hours of processing time that could be used by somebody else with no negative impact on Southwestern. Woods was intrigued with the idea and, since there was no obvious downside for him, agreed to provide his organisation's excess capacity and split any profits with Perot.

Armed with a launch platform, Perot wasted no time in finding a buyer. He began calling every company in the US that had recently bought an IBM 7070 mainframe, of which there were 110, to see if any of them wanted more processing time. The 78th company on the list, Collins Radio, said that they did and, most importantly, would be willing to pay for it. A deal was struck and for two months people and magnetic tape (containing data) shuttled back and forth between Dallas and Cedar Rapids.

Perot banked $100,000 (the equivalent of $1 m in 2024).

Perot's second deal—with the Agricultural Commodity Price Stabilisation Service—confirmed the viability of his idea and provided the foundation to expand. He hired his first employee, Betty Taylor, as his secretary, then three former IBM colleagues—Mitch Hart, Tom Marquez and Jim Cole. Perot knew where every IBM mainframe in the Dallas area was located—since he himself had sold most of them—and started negotiations with the owners to lease excess capacity while his small band of salespeople went looking for customers. When Marquez sold a deal to Frito-Lay in early 1963, EDS was firmly established on the road to success.

That was when Perot made his next incremental innovation. He realised that his small, but growing, customer base were all from different industries. That wasn't a problem per se, but it meant that each was unique, with needs that were correspondingly unique. Perot guessed that, if he could sell computer systems to companies within the same industry, there would be commonalities in their computer system needs, and as a result they would be easier to service. As luck would have it, the Dallas area had a plethora of insurance companies that all operated according to the same government mandated standards. Mitch Hart was tasked with selling to local companies and soon established a small customer base of insurance industry customers, all of whom were running similar processes. Perot soon discovered that his assumption was correct: it was much easier—and less expensive—to support organisations with similar needs, and this translated into more money to the bottom line of EDS's finances.

EDS continued to go from strength to strength over the next couple of years—attracting new customers, expanding outside of the Dallas-Fort Worth metroplex and building a reputation for excellent customer service—consistently under promising and over delivering.

But, operational cracks were appearing. It was proving to be a business that was heavily dependent on people, and finding good people was difficult. By now, EDS wasn't just brokering computer time-sharing deals, it was building technology solutions that comprised hardware, software and services, and making heavy use of computer engineers, programmers and operators. It had even started its own training initiative—the EDS Systems Engineer Development Program[57]—but, as the business grew, demand for talent was continually outstripping supply. The problem came to a head in February 1969 when two EDS'ers, Mort Meyerson and Mitch Hart, were in Camp Hill trying to close a deal with Pennsylvania Blue Shield.

The prospective customer was struggling to conform to government legislation to provide low-cost health insurance to the aged and disabled. It was well staffed, well funded and well managed, but exhibited poor performance on a range of metrics, most critically unprocessed claims. On the surface this looked like a great opportunity for EDS since they had established experience with the government regulations via other customers and would be able to bring that expertise to Pennsylvania Blue Shield. But, EDS simply didn't have the people available to staff a new account. As Meyerson and Hart discussed the problem one morning over breakfast, they came up with an entirely new concept. This time, it wasn't an incremental innovation, it was a big, transformative and fundamental tsunami innovation.

Their idea was to transition Pennsylvania Blue Shield's entire computer department to EDS—systems, software and even people. EDS would then inject a contingent of systems engineers with appropriate experience to upgrade performance and bring the department in line with government standards: a truly revolutionary approach that had never been done before! A few days later, despite the idea still having a slew of unknowns, an agreement was reached. EDS acquired eighty-six new employees, and an entirely new business—*IT outsourcing*[58]—was invented. As a postscript, Pennsylvania Blue Shield were in full compliance with government standards four months later.

The story of EDS highlights two key aspects of incremental innovation. First, small manageable adjustments to any model can have huge, far-reaching consequences. Second, continual incremental innovation builds a tolerance for change that increases the ability to tolerate occasional fundamental transformation.

Incremental innovation is applicable in any group initiative, but particularly well suited to collaborative endeavours. There's something about bringing together a diverse group of people to collectively achieve a purpose that creates a natural foundation for the identification, creation, exploration and adoption of new ideas. The more challenging the target outcome, the more open collaborative communities usually are to innovative new concepts. Co-creation and positive peer pressure is a driver of success, and collaborative endeavours—with a mix of talent—are fertile ground for fresh thinking.

And the best part is, not only is incremental innovation a manageable form of transformation, it can also be introduced to a collaborative endeavour in manageable stages.

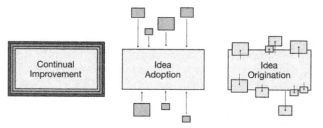

As a first step, it can be focused on **continual improvement:** looking for small ways to enhance different aspects of the endeavour—tools, processes, techniques, activities, resources—and then selectively implementing the best ideas.[59] This approach requires a minimal investment of time and effort but still stimulates the creativity and engagement of participants. It's a highly accessible form of incremental innovation that favours small changes that are quick and easy to adopt.

When the drive for continual improvement becomes ingrained within a community, and a general tolerance for change increases, the next stage of incremental innovation is **external idea adoption**. The focus here is on actively looking for new ideas that can be applied to the endeavour. Some ideas may be brought by participants leveraging prior experience on other initiatives, whereas others can be based on new concepts that participants have heard about, but have no tangible experience of.

Whether or not there is any pre-existing experience within the community, external idea adoption is a low-risk approach to innovation because the ideas in question are at least partially pre-constructed and core research and development has been done elsewhere. Potential impact can also be relatively easily considered before and during implementation, with progress monitored and managed for maximum value and minimal disruption. Overall, it's an efficient and effective method of delving deeper into innovation and helps to keep a collaborative endeavour *continuously contemporary*™—always adapting to current circumstances and always taking advantage of breakthrough thinking.

The third level of incremental innovation is **internal idea origination**, where breakthrough thinking is cultivated from within the collaborative community.[60] Instead of adopting externally originated ideas, this taps directly into the expertise and creativity of the collaborative community itself, to develop proprietary ideas that can deliver significant and defensible advantage. The focus expands from keeping the endeavour continuously contemporary™ through secondary innovation, to making it *perpetually prospicient*™ through primary innovation. In the process, the endeavour is better positioned for addressing tomorrow's challenges.

Internal idea origination is a significant step-up and is much more challenging to cultivate. But, if focus is maintained on micro- rather than mega-transformation, it is well within the capabilities of most collaborative endeavours. This doesn't mean that creativity has to be restricted or stifled in any way; if big ideas in the form of fundamental innovation come to light, they should always be carefully considered for development. But, effort and expectations should be biased towards developing ideas leading to manageable change that can be implemented without significant disruption.

To create an environment in which incremental innovation can be cultivated, there are four conditions that it's important to establish.

The first is to **breakdown organisational barriers** and enable all voices to be heard, regardless of seniority or experience. To do this, internal structures have to be flexible enough that even the

> **Cultivating an Innovative Environment**
>
> Break Organisational Barriers
> Create Urgency
> Challenge Assumptions
> Embrace Failure

most junior people can find a platform for their ideas. It's a difficult condition to nurture in traditional organisations where deeply embedded hierarchical structures have a tendency to suppress ideas and opinions that are outside of the ordinary. But, it's something that can be relatively easily created in collaborative endeavours, where the organisational structure is founded on the need for specific capabilities and achievement of a community-based statement of purpose. How participants are organised to deliver those capabilities is based on how best to arrange them in order to achieve the target outcome rather than any pre-conceived standards or ideals. Inevitably, there will be some kind of hierarchy in every endeavour, and some participants will play a more senior role than others, but there is an inbuilt capacity for the intermingling of concepts and opinions that tends to stimulate a broader outlook than in more traditional environments.

The second condition is to **create a sense of urgency**. This is obvious in situations where the endeavour has fallen behind schedule and it is therefore essential to establish a group-level intolerance for missed milestones. But, it's also useful even when the endeavour is proceeding smoothly and achieving targets on time and on budget. This is because, although innovation can be borne out of stability—get it right and then make it better—it more often emerges from adversity and challenge. And, an easy way to introduce an element of challenge is to regularly review goals and apply pressure to achieve them faster. It's a manageable method of introducing tension within the community, ensuring that participants don't relax when everything seems to be on track and proceeding as expected.

A third condition to institute is a willingness to **challenge core assumptions**. This is a less extreme version of the philosophy of "*if it ain't broke, break it*", and involves encouraging people at all levels to constantly question "*Why are we doing things this way?*" and "*What are the factors that are driving us?*" The intent isn't to arbitrarily undermine legitimate beliefs or disregard core drivers, but to challenge them and check their validity in a constantly evolving environment. Assumptions that are easily defended, with clear arguments for their validity, will probably be reasonable and should be accepted. But, those that are less easily defended and prone to convoluted argument are areas to look at more closely. In all instances, an environment in which traditional mores are occasionally questioned adds another useful layer of creative tension.

The fourth and final condition to instil in an innovative collaborative community is to openly and actively **embrace failure**. This is important because one of the less appealing but unavoidable attributes of innovation is that the final outcome is uncertain. It doesn't matter how much effort is put into pre-developing new ideas and considering all possibilities, some *will* be unsuccessful. But, this can't be allowed to be a barrier to creativity. If success is held up as the only acceptable option, rather than cultivating an environment of excellence it will do the exact opposite; it will discourage people from trying anything that involves any element of stretch and will fuel a drive to mediocrity. Occasional failure has to be perceived as not just acceptable, but desirable. It builds experience and perseverance and can be a key driver of innovation when successful ideas in one area emerge from failures in another. In fact, one of the tests of the true innovative nature of a group is the number of failures that it generates.

But, it has to be recognised that while establishing the right conditions for innovation is an essential foundation, it is not an automatic guarantee that interesting new ideas will emerge. In the right environment, innovation can appear spontaneously and can originate from anywhere at any time. But, to maximise that probability it's useful to actively cultivate innovative thinking and then nurture ideas as they appear. This is done by introducing innovation springboards that push participants to accept new concepts as a central aspect of their day-to-day responsibilities.

A good starting springboard, is to look at the **existing challenges** facing the endeavour—orchestrating discussions where participants present the key problems that they are facing and how they're addressing them. The community can then respond with feedback or provide suggestions for alternatives. This is a very tangible and pragmatic approach to innovation and keeps it grounded in the here and now. It means that those participants who are less open to, or practiced in, innovative thinking can flex a little, but still remain close to familiar boundaries. It embeds a seed of innovative thinking while simultaneously encouraging cross-endeavour relationships and helping participants feel that they are part of something bigger than just their immediate area of responsibility.

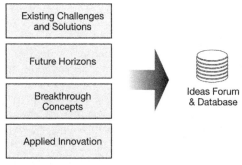

A more advanced springboard is to move people beyond thinking about the here and now to thinking about the future. Initially, this doesn't have to be with the explicit goal of finding actionable innovation: it can simply be to stretch thinking—understanding how the world is changing and considering what might be necessary to react to those changes. A good way to do this is to conduct **future horizons** discussions, where people talk about what they think might happen over two distinct time horizons. Those horizons are dependent on the endeavour, but two that often seem to work well are twelve months and five years.[61] The twelve-month horizon is near term and keeps people focused on dynamics that are relevant right now and how they might affect either the endeavour or its target outcome. The five-year horizon encourages more expansive thinking since it is usually beyond the immediate scope of the endeavour but still within a realistic and understandable timeframe for most participants.

A more pioneering innovation springboard is to proactively seek new ideas and get people thinking about new concepts that might be relevant to the endeavour. One way to do this is through **breakthrough concepts** sessions, where participants share intriguing new ideas they've encountered or heard about. These ideas don't need to be directly relevant to the current endeavour, and the only prerequisite is that they are interesting. Such discussions offer a lightweight and fun respite from the daily grind of meeting deliverables and milestones, while gently and subtly increasing the culture of innovation.[62]

A more direct approach is with **applied innovation** sessions. These are more tangible and are explicitly aimed at identifying and discussing ideas that have the potential to directly influence an endeavour. The ideas that emerge from these sessions may develop from previous conversation—such as around challenges or anticipated future trends—or they may be spontaneously conceived by participants. And, they can originate from external sources (idea adoption) or within the community (idea origination). In all instances, the overarching objective is to more deeply embed an innovative culture within the endeavour by encouraging participants to share ideas that they believe can deliver a positive impact.

No matter how ideas are cultivated within a collaborative community, it's a good approach to, first, place them in an ideas forum or incubator, where they can undergo further scrutiny. Within the forum, they can be explored, expanded on, and allowed to develop into tangible innovations capable of implementation. It also provides the necessary time and space to evolve, and good ideas will rise to the top as their viability becomes increasingly apparent through discussion and refinement. Those ideas that don't reach the top of the forum can still hold value and be the source of spin-off innovation; if there is enough capacity and interest, they can be selected for limited support or allowed to develop as side projects.

For those ideas that do rise to the top, the best way to assess them for implementation is to think about them in terms of a value equation.

Value = Benefits - Costs

In simple terms, the equation outlines that, if the benefits of the idea outweigh the cost, then it should be considered for implementation. If not, it should be deprioritised and returned to the ideas forum, at least for now.

For most ideas, the core elements of the value equation are reasonably clear. The benefit is the problem or opportunity that will be addressed by the idea, and the cost is the price of implementation. But, there are also some less obvious, extended benefits and costs that should be considered: for example, an often overlooked extended cost that is ongoing, or support fees that may come from implementing an idea.

A good way to ensure that the majority of benefits and costs are considered, is to think about them within six categories:

- **Logistical:** is concerned with the impact on assets, including material, materiel and personnel.
- **Financial:** is concerned with the impact on economics, including immediate and recurring fees and income.
- **Informational:** is concerned with the impact on knowledge, including added complexity, training and development, experience and expertise.
- **Political:** is concerned with the impact on reputation, including status, brand, influence and power.
- **Social:** is concerned with the impact on relationships, including motivation, engagement and enthusiasm.
- **Temporal:** is concerned with the impact on timelines, including milestones, dependencies and outcomes.

Every idea will come with benefits and costs across all six areas. Investing the time to clarify them, and to develop the value equation beyond the immediately obvious, reduces the likelihood that an idea will progress to implementation before the full true costs have been understood. It also minimises the chance that a great idea is rejected because the costs were clear but the extended benefits were not. While the units of measurement are never consistent between categories, it's usually possible to make an educated and reasonable assessment of whether the benefits of implementation outweigh and justify the costs.

But, the value equation is just a first gate. Two further gates should be considered as an idea moves along the path to implementation. The first of these is whether the collaborative community is capable of implementing the idea, and the second is whether it has the capacity to do so.

1. Do the benefits of the idea outweigh the costs?
   a. If "yes" proceed to step 2.
   b. If "no" deprioritise the idea.
2. Does the community have the capability to implement the idea?
   a. If "yes" proceed to step 3.
   b. If "no" do the benefits of the idea warrant acquiring the capability?
      i. If "yes" proceed to step 3.
      ii. If "no" deprioritise the idea.
3. Does the community have the capacity to implement the idea?
   a. If "yes" assemble or acquire the required capability and IMPLEMENT.
   b. If "no" do the benefits of the idea warrant increasing or reallocating capacity?
      i. If "yes" increase or reallocate capacity, assemble or acquire the required capability, and IMPLEMENT.
      ii. If "no" deprioritise the idea.

To progress to full implementation, all three gates should be cleared. And, even after an idea has successfully navigated all three, it can still be prudent to conduct an initial limited implementation—especially for ideas carrying significant risks or high costs. This won't work for every idea, and some will require full commitment from the outset, but for most it's sensible to run pilot programmes first then move to full implementation once the value of the idea has been confirmed.

By that point, the idea will have completed the full evolution from concept to idea to innovation to transformation, and the chances of its successful implementation will be high.

The core challenge when inculcating a culture of innovation within a collaborative community is that the structured nature of the endeavour can seem to be at odds with the nature of innovation which, by definition, is disruptive and thrives on disorder and uncertainty; it is the product of people thinking creatively, adapting swiftly, and accepting unconventional answers to questions. And yet, well-orchestrated endeavours typically process along relatively clearly defined paths towards a target outcome—where disorder is anathema.

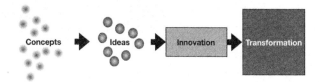

But, the two don't have to be mutually exclusive. The secret is to cultivate an environment where people are given structure and process, but also allowed the freedom and encouragement to explore concepts and develop them into ideas that are potentially paradigm-shifting. While the endeavour itself is carefully orchestrated, this doesn't mean that it should be allowed to become entrenched in day-to-day responsibilities. Instead, it should embrace fresh thinking and actively look for ways to reach the target outcome faster, cheaper or more effectively. New ideas should be nurtured into innovations, and the innovations should be pushed into transformation.

The Apollo Program

You'd be forgiven for thinking that the Apollo program was the definitive source of all innovation that came into general use in the second half of the 20th century. After all, there have been thousands of articles listing the amazing products that

La Lune - Image courtesy: Roger Alderson

emerged from the program. But, although the Apollo program certainly took advantage of the most advanced research and innovative thinking of the time, it wasn't the source of most of the inventions that have been erroneously attributed to it. To illustrate, here are a few examples of innovations that have been incorrectly attributed to the Apollo program:

- **Liquid Cooled Garments:** invented by the Royal Academy of Engineering for the Royal Air Force, in 1959.
- **Integrated Circuits:** invented by (Nobel prize winner) Jack Kilby at Texas Instruments, in 1958, and patented in 1959; then further refined (into the monolithic IC) by Robert Noyce of Fairchild Semiconductor, in 1960.
- **Flameproof Clothing (aromatic polybenzimidazole):** invented by Carl Shipp Marvel for the US Air Force, in 1955.
- **Velcro:** invented by George de Mestral, in 1941.
- **PTFE (aka Teflon):** invented by Roy J. Plunkett at DuPont, in 1938.
- **The Quartz Clock:** invented by Joseph W. Horton and Warren A. Marrison at Bell Telephone Laboratories, in 1927 (based on research by Jacques and Pierre Curie in 1880).
- **Fly-By-Wire Vehicles:** first tested in the Tupolev ANT-20 aircraft, in 1933. Patented by Karl Otto Altvater for Siemens in 1934 and first applied in a non-experimental aircraft (the Avro Canada CF-105 Arrow) in 1958.
- **Solar Cell:** invented by Edmond Becquerel, in 1839 (when he was just 19).

- **Freeze Dried Food:** invented by the Inca[63] in the 13th century when they freeze dried potatoes into chuño, but modernised in 1890 by Prussian pathologist and histologist, Richard Altmann.

In reality, only a handful of inventions can be genuinely attributed to the Apollo program for their origin: scratch resistant lenses (developed by Foster Grant for space suit visors), building shock absorbers (developed by Taylor Devices for rocket launch buildings), battery-powered hand-held tools (developed by Black and Decker for a lunar drill) and the moon blanket.

But, while the Apollo program may not have been the initial source of much of the innovation it utilised, it was the poster child for applied innovation in the form of idea adoption and refinement. Faced with incredibly aggressive timelines, Apollo teams were always looking for solutions to the myriad of challenges that they faced, and were quick to adopt ideas that could be effectively applied to their unique circumstances. They didn't invent Teflon, Velcro, aromatic polybenzimidazole or liquid cooled garments, but they were quick to adopt, adapt and apply them for space suits. They didn't invent fly-by-wire aircraft, but they refined the technology to the point that the lunar lander was the first purely electronic fly-by-wire aircraft with control managed through a computer and no mechanical or hydraulic backup. They didn't even invent rocket engines, but they pushed them to new levels that were, genuinely, out of this world!

There are thousands of examples of how the Apollo program embraced incremental innovation, but one of the most compelling, is the story of the Apollo guidance computer.

The story begins in 1957, when the Massachusetts Institute of Technology Instrumentation Laboratory, while working on a US Air project, undertook some *"relevant independent research"* into a space guidance system based on a hypothetical journey of a spacecraft to Mars. For a side project, the work was incredibly rigorous, and by mid-1959 the team had assembled a four-volume set of descriptions and diagrams that comprehensively detailed a hypothetical spacecraft, a computer and associated support systems. Understandably proud of their work, they showed it to their client who was complementary but not particularly interested and suggested that they try the newly formed space agency, NASA.

The team secured a meeting with the Deputy Administrator of NASA, Hugh Dryden, and he *was* interested; a formative relationship was established. In April 1961, Kennedy announced an ambition to send a man to the Moon and eleven weeks later, the MIT Instrumentation Lab signed one of the first prime contractor agreements with NASA, taking responsibility for designing and building the lunar guidance and navigation system.

It was the hypothetical work that MIT had conducted back in 1957 that equipped them to win the contract. They'd recognised then that limitations in radio transmission meant that a spacecraft travelling vast distances from Earth would be impossible to control via Earth-based systems. So, to get their imaginary spacecraft to Mars, they'd designed an autonomous system that consisted of an onboard general-purpose computer with pre-wired, read-only memory.

For the real-world trip to the Moon (and back), autonomous onboard guidance was exactly what was needed and the MIT Instrumentation Lab had already done a lot of thinking for what would be required. They combined this thinking with emerging innovations that could help them achieve their goal, most notably the integrated circuit. It was truly bleeding-edge technology: invented in 1958, patented in 1959 and refined in 1960. In late 1961, as they started to sketch out their ideas for the lunar guidance and navigation system, MIT saw the enormous potential of the integrated circuit—particularly its minimal size and weight—and partnered with Fairchild Semiconductor to use it in the AGC —the Apollo Guidance Computer.

As the decade progressed, the design was continually refined. It used all known methods of obtaining navigation data (inertial, celestial, radar and ground tracking) and consisted of an inertial measurement unit, a computational unit and an optical unit. It included a user interface so that astronauts could examine navigational, guidance and control data, and even update it if necessary. MIT designed the system and assembled the software, but parts were manufactured by AC Sparkplug (for the inertial system), Raytheon (for guidance computers) and Kollsman Instrument Company (for optics).

During bench testing, the unit performed as expected, but it wasn't fully tested until Apollo 8 flew to the Moon and back. That mission performed eight revolutions of the Moon, and during the periods when it was on the far side, it had no contact with Earth and no tracking information. The AGC performed flawlessly, and continued to perform flawlessly for every subsequent Apollo mission.

An interesting postscript to this story is about one of the Fairchild Semiconductor managers at the time—a man called Gordon Moore. In an article published in 'Electronics Magazine' on 19 April 1965, Moore was asked to forecast what might happen to the semiconductor industry over the next few years. He predicted that the number of components on an integrated circuit would double every year.[64] His prediction, astounding at the time, turned out to be correct. Indeed, although the AGC performed its task flawlessly for the Apollo program, by the time it was used to get Armstrong, Aldrin and Collins to the Moon in 1969, it was already painfully obsolete technology!

The Apollo Guidance Computer, and MIT's intensely collaborative work on it, is a great example of how strong and effective the culture of innovation was at NASA during the 1960s. NASA and its collaborators continually found, assessed and adopted thousands of diverse new ideas that they then adjusted and refined for specific purposes, before successfully integrating them within the initiative. And, it wasn't just physical items: they were simultaneously developing new approaches and processes for everything from human resource management to partner relations. There is probably no greater example of how to establish and maintain a culture of continuous incremental innovation, than the Apollo program.

Epilogue
(aka Orchestrate)

Collaboration doesn't just ... happen!

In closing this book, there's one final point to make: collaboration doesn't simply emerge organically.

It's a natural part of our existence, and deeply ingrained into human nature, but people working together for mutual gain is something that must still be nurtured. The *right* people with the *right* skills at the *right* time in the *right* place have a strong chance of achieving the *right* target outcome, but only if they have appropriate support, guidance and... orchestration.[65]

Collaborative orchestration draws on many aspects of what would be generally recognised as project management and deals with deliverables, milestones, timescales, resource allocations, task dependencies and critical paths. But, collaboration orchestrators also deal with engagement,

> *Orchestrators are the **fuel** to power the collaboration engine, the **lubricant** to minimise friction within it, and the **connectivity** and linkage to ensure that all of the components work together and produce forward momentum.*

performance, contribution, problem management and esprit de corps. They optimise the collaborative environment and act as the catalyst to bring everything together and drive an endeavour to success.

Unsurprisingly, being able to do this is challenging, and effective collaborative orchestration requires strong capabilities in a variety of areas—with seven key skills being of particular importance.

The first—and most obvious—skill is to be well **organised**: capable of effectively arranging personal responsibilities associated with an endeavour and, when necessary, arranging the responsibilities of other participants too. To do this, good orchestrators typically:

- Use calendars and scheduling tools to compartmentalise time into well-defined blocks within which activities can be effectively undertaken.
- Continually develop and update task lists that ensure that high-priority activities get the most attention, and those that are of lower priority are minimised or ignored altogether.
- Optimise workflows through techniques such as process standardisation, batch processing and task automation.

The second key skill of an orchestrator is to be **results oriented**, with a very deliberate focus on those activities that tangibly support achieving the outcome of an endeavour. This means:

- Maintaining an acute awareness of individual and collective goals including: the paths required to undertake them, the potential barriers to achieving them, and the progress made towards completing them.
- Continually assessing activities into categories of: *do* (for those that are quick and simple to complete), *defer* (for those that are more involved), *delegate* (for those that can be passed to others) or *delete* (for those that can be abandoned).

- Accepting occasional imperfections and refusing to allow 'great' to be the enemy of 'good'.

    The third key orchestration skill is to be **decisive**, with a willingness to accept responsibility for important decisions—including an ability to make difficult or unpopular choices when necessary. To do this, orchestrators need to:

- Accept full responsibility for an endeavour—including accountability for its success or failure—understanding that consensus is not always possible and tie-breaking decisions will be required.
- Strive for data-driven decisions based on objective evaluation of progress and performance whenever possible, but accept that intuitive-driven decisions will occasionally be necessary.
- Quickly address issues and harness all available resources to overcome them.

    The fourth orchestration skill is to be **intellectually agile**, with the flexibility to consider multiple options and ideas. This means:

- Assembling and disseminating all available relevant information that increases knowledge and understanding across the entire collaborative community.
- Questioning conventional assumptions, especially those that are restrictive or inhibiting.
- Actively encouraging the exploration of new ideas and paradigms that could be adopted to achieve the outcome of the endeavour cheaper, faster, or more effectively.

    The fifth skill of an orchestrator is to be **people-oriented**, with an ability to cultivate enduring personal relationships and to facilitate relationships between others. To do this they:

- Look for common interests and attitudes as the fundamental foundation for bringing people together.
- Place an inordinately high priority on trust, with an absolute commitment to consistency, reliability and honesty in all aspects of relationships.

- Give and take, understanding that strong relationships are bidirectional and people value both reward and contribution.

The sixth skill is **self-awareness**, with a comprehensive understanding of personal strengths and weaknesses. This means:

- Recognising and balancing personal beliefs and biases that could impact performance—both positive and negative.
- Mitigating weaknesses by: accessing the expertise of others, using relevant tools and undertaking focused personal development.
- Channelling emotions and ego so that they enable rather than obstruct progress and performance.

The final skill that orchestrators should possess is **emotional intelligence**—an ability to recognise, understand, accept and influence the feelings of others. This means:

- Empathising with others, relating to their unique perspectives and appreciating the challenges that they face.
- Understanding that there are different working styles, and striving to create the conditions that allow individuals to feel respected, valued and capable of contributing to the best of their ability.
- Using positive reinforcement and recognition to encourage and motivate high-performance contribution.

It isn't essential for an orchestrator to be an expert in all seven key skills, but it is necessary to possess a reasonably high degree of competence in each of them; the greater the competence, the more effective the orchestration will be. Orchestrators who can apply all of the skills will ensure the best possible allocation of time, effort and resources on those activities that are most critical for success. The more skilled and experienced the orchestrator is, the more capable they will be of shepherding the endeavour to achieving its purpose.

Of course, building orchestration skills, like any other skills, takes time and effort. Even the very best orchestrators are continually looking for ways to further develop their capabilities: this can involve formal training, but informal learning opportunities play an important role too. Observing best practice in others, listening to feedback, reviewing personal performance and undertaking self-directed exploration are all excellent ways of building expertise. In a constantly evolving world, lifelong learning is no longer a choice: it's a necessity for maintaining currency and relevance.

TLDR

There are three reasons why you may be reading this chapter of the book. First, because you're the type of person who devours every word in a book, in which case you'll probably read through the glossary too. Second, you've already read the entire book, but now want a summary to refer back to as you apply some of the principles within it. Third, you don't have the time or the inclination to read the full book, and just want a quick reference that you can use to learn a little more about principles of collaboration without getting embroiled in the boring details.

No judgement from me. Whichever of the three reasons drove you here, the following pages summarise all of the content contained in the preceding pages.

I hope that you find it useful.

FORMULATE

Components of a statement of purpose:
- Vision - brief narrative describing a target outcome.
- Motivation - reason(s) for achieving a target outcome.
- Timescale - timeframe to achieve a target outcome.

Attributes of a goal:
- Specificity - *what* must be achieved, by *how much*, and *when*.
- Relevance - alignment to purpose.
- Attainability - is it realistically possible.
- Attribution - assigned ownership.

Goal difficulty/attainability ranking:
- Manageable - relatively easy.
- Demanding - somewhat difficult.
- Challenging - extremely difficult.
- Formidable - arduous.

ASSOCIATE

Capability types:
- Functional - essential fundamental capabilities.
- Organisational - optional supporting capabilities.
- Informational - internal/external communication capabilities.

Categories of capability significance:
- Essential - must have.
- Consequential - should have.
- Valuable - nice to have.
- Useful - optional.

Categories of capability urgency:
- Exigent - immediately required.
- Acute - imminently required.
- Pressing - near-term required.
- Liminal - long-term or optionally required.

Contact network types:
- Immediate - friends, family and current colleagues.
- Direct - acquaintances and former colleagues.
- Adjacent Indirect - networks of friends, family, colleagues and acquaintances.
- Indirect - no connection.

Collaborator attributes:
- Primary:

- Ability - appropriate experience, expertise or perspective.
- Bandwidth - capacity to participate.
- Interest - motivation to participate.
- Secondary:
  - Affinity - cultural, emotional and intellectual alignment.
  - Perspective - broad outlook of attitude and understanding.
  - Tolerance - appreciation of alternative perspectives.
  - Drive - propensity for action.
  - Situational Awareness - awareness of internal and external dynamics.
  - Flexibility - willingness to flex based on changing situations.
  - Eloquence - capable of clear and concise communications.
  - Integrity - reputation for honesty and integrity.

Elements of a collaborator agreement:
- Obligations - role and responsibilities of each party.
- Term and Termination - the expected duration of the relationship and the conditions for ending it.
- Confidentiality - restrictions to disclosure of information regarding the endeavour.
- Financial Factors - details on funding, investment and revenue sharing.
- Intellectual Property - clarification of ownership of intellectual inputs and outputs.
- Project Management - outlining the project management approach.
- Exclusivity - restrictions on performing the same or similar work, or working with competitors.
- Non-solicitation - guidelines for extra-endeavour relationship management.
- Documents, Records and Data Protection - how records and documents (including personal data) will be handled.
- Dispute Resolution: provisions for resolving disagreements.
- Liability - limitations on legal, financial and asset obligations.

Attributes of a collaborative environment:
- Arena - a space to talk, explore ideas, build understanding, resolve issues and draw conclusions.
- Lexicon - a repository of terms and expressions relevant to an endeavour.
- Guiding Principles - the core standards and fundamental rules of participation.

ACTIVATE

A collaborative action plan consists of a hierarchy of interrelated
actions in the form of:
* Goals.
    * Approaches.
        * Tasks.
            * Activities.

Questions to consider when assessing the risk of an action:
* How severe are the consequences of failure and will it stifle or
  inhibit other opportunities, either now or in the future?
* When undertaking the action will it:
    * Conflict with other actions?
    * Bring challenges that are difficult to predict, mitigate, control
      and overcome?
    * Require difficult access to assets?

Questions to consider when assessing the benefit of an action:
* How substantial are the benefits of success and will it spawn other
  opportunities and expand options, either now or in the future?
* When undertaking the action will it:
    * Complement other actions?
    * Bring challenges that are straightforward to predict, mitigate,
      control and overcome?
    * Require easy access to assets?

Categories of risk:
* Perilous - potentially catastrophic.
* Consequential - far-reaching.
* Nominal - Somewhat negative.
* Minimal - low impact.

Categories of reward:
* Invaluable - substantial.
* Beneficial - significant.
* Marginal - positive.
* Limited - minimal.

To define and sequence an action list:
* Interdependencies - how actions relate to one another.
* Constraints - factors that impact action sequencing.
* Resource Requirements - core needs in terms of human capital,
  raw materials, equipment, technology, tools and finance.
* Ownership - the individuals or groups responsible for
  implementing an action.

- Risks and Mitigations - threats to success and methods of minimisation.

EVALUATE

Key operational metrics:
- Schedule - the achievement of milestones and checkpoints.
- Budget - alignment with financial projections.
- Quality - standards for deliverables.
- Resource Utilisation - consumption rates of equipment and supplies.
- Effort - work levels of individuals and teams.

Key behavioural metrics:
- Contribution - meeting, missing, or exceeding assigned responsibilities.
- Communication - maintaining open, transparent and free-flowing communication.
- Confidence - showing enthusiasm, optimism and belief in the target outcome.

NES (Net Engagement Score™):
A measure of participant engagement in an endeavour based on analysis of individual answers to the question *"How do you perceive progress of the endeavour?"*

MOTIVATE

Bruce Tuckman's stages of group development:
- Forming - coming together around a defined purpose.
- Storming - stabilisation as relationships solidify.
- Norming - establishing clarity of purpose and action.
- Performing - focusing on achieving the target outcome.

Principles/attributes of a high-performing collaborate community:
- Strong Sense of Direction - everybody having the same target outcome in mind.
- Unimpeded Information - clear communication channels up, down and across the organisation.
- Appropriate Resources - appropriate tools and materials to fulfil responsibilities.
- No Roadblocks - minimal distractions and barriers to performance.
- Commitment Confidence - a culture where promises are expected to be kept.
- Opportunities for Growth - taking advantage of opportunities to build expertise and experience.

- Performance Acknowledgement - recognising and rewarding contribution.

MEDIATE

Types of mediation:
- Avoid - wait for an issue to go away or resolve itself.
- Accommodate - play down tensions and sooth egos.
- Confront - get to the least-worst option.
- Compromise - find an acceptable middle ground.

Steps of Integrative mediation:
- Set the Environment - clarify roles, advocate compromise, assign timescales and agree ground rules.
- Explore Issues - define problems and positions.
- Reach for Resolution - identify options, prioritise and select the most appropriate resolution.

INNOVATE

Types of innovation:
- Fundamental - groundbreaking ideas leading to 'chasm transformation' that is revolutionary in scope.
- Incremental - small but meaningful ideas leading to 'crevasse transformation' that is evolutionary in scope.

Incremental innovation stages:
- Continual Improvement - small enhancements to existing tools, processes, techniques, activities or resources.
- External Idea Adoption - adopting and adapting externally developed ideas.
- Internal Idea Origination - encouraging and nurturing internally development breakthrough thinking.

Actions to foster a culture of innovation:
- Breakdown Organisational Barriers - provide a non-hierarchical ideas platform.
- Drive Urgency - continually push timelines.
- Challenge Assumptions - do not accept the status quo.
- Embrace Failure - encourage (measured) risk-taking.

Innovation springboards:
- Challenge Resolutions - actively discuss challenges and solutions.
- Future Considerations - think about how the world is changing and what might happen in the near- and mid-term.
- New Ideas Exploration and Inculcation - look internally and externally for interesting and relevant new ideas.

Idea Value = Benefits - Costs

Benefits and costs categories:
- Logistical - assets, including material, materiel and personnel.
- Financial - economics, including fees and income, direct, support and maintenance.
- Informational - knowledge, including added complexity, training and development, understanding, experience and expertise.
- Political - reputation, including status (brand), influence and power.
- Social - relationships, including motivation, engagement and enthusiasm.
- Temporal - timelines, including milestones, dependencies and outcomes.

ORCHESTRATE

Key orchestration skills:
- Organised - effectively arranging responsibilities.
- Results Oriented - focusing on the most relevant activities.
- Decisive - willing and able to make decisions.
- Intellectually Agile - always willing to consider new ideas and approaches.
- People-Oriented - able to establish and maintain relationships.
- Self-Aware - cognisant of personal strengths and weaknesses.
- Emotionally Intelligent - able to recognise, understand, accept and influence the feelings of others.

Glossary

Action	An approach, task or activity that could be undertaken in the pursuit of a target outcome.
Activity	An action that, when combined with other activities, could achieve a task.
Approach	An action that could achieve a goal.
Collaborator/Participant	An individual or organisation working with others to achieve a purpose.
Community	A group of individuals and/or organisations working together to achieve a purpose.
Coordination	Organising, managing and facilitating a collaborative endeavour.
Endeavour	An initiative involving multiple individuals and/or organisations working together to achieve a purpose.
Goal	A strategic target that must be completed to achieve a purpose.
Idea Adoption	The act of recognising interesting ideas from outside and adapting them to be relevant to a group.
Idea Origination	The act of cultivating ideas from within a group.
Innovation	New ideas, products, services, tools, processes, or techniques that have the potential to drive positive change and create value.

Innovation Exhaust	Interesting new ideas that emerge as a tangential by-product of innovative thinking.
Innovation Springboard	An orchestrated activity intended to propel participants in an endeavour to find interesting and innovative ideas.
Micro-Productivity	The concept of successfully undertaking multiple small tasks as a driver of success.
Micro-Transformation	Implementing relatively small ideas (incremental innovation) as a component of positive transformation.
Orchestrator/Administrator	The individual or organisation responsible for managing a collaborative endeavour.
PMO/PCO	Program Management Office/Program Coordination Office. A formal organisational function charged with responsibility for project managing a collaborative endeavour.
Purpose [Statement of]	A clear, concise and engaging description of the target outcome of a collaborative endeavour with vision, timeframe and meaning components.
Significance	The reason(s) that a collaborative endeavour is important.
Strategy	An approach that has been selected for implementation.
Tactic	A task that has been selected for implementation.

Task	An action that, when combined with other tasks, could achieve an approach.
Transformation	The process of undertaking positive change to create value.
Vision	A clear description of the target outcome of a collaborative endeavour.

Notes

1   In 1657, Blaise Pascal wrote, "Je n'ai fait celle-ci plus longue que parce que je n'ai pas eu le loisir de la faire plus courte". A modern day translation would be, "I have made this longer than usual because I have not had time to make it shorter".

2   It's essential to define a timeline for the achievement of any goal. Effort will expand or contract to fit the timeline so this should be the shortest possible PRACTICAL timescale.

3   Often a group can reach consensus of the importance of each goal, simply through discussion. But, if this isn't possible, each participant can provide their own individual assessment which can then be consolidated and averaged to create a collective grade for each goal.

4   It can be useful to occasionally reach out to people who are not directly involved in the endeavour for unbiased and pragmatic perspectives. In this way, small (but potentially important) goal nuances can be identified and explored.

5   The significance/urgency model also provides insight into thinking about gaps and overlaps, a consideration that is especially important for capabilities in the top right of the model where there should be very few capability gaps since the absence of just one could lead to the failure of an entire endeavour. Similarly, occasional overlaps, where more than one collaborator can bring the same capability, are useful in reducing risk.

6   The motive for participation could be simply a sense of personal reward, but while altruism is a possible motivation, it's very rare.

7   Adaptation from Shakespeare's The Tempest, "Misery acquaints a man with strange bedfellows", spoken by a shipwrecked man who takes shelter beside a sleeping monster.

8   Compromising on the integrity of collaborators is rarely a good idea and should only be considered in exceptional (typically existential) circumstances.

9   It can also be useful to consider the potential for neurodiversity within a collaborative community. With an estimated 15-20 percent of people exhibiting some form of neurodivergence, understanding and embracing cognitively diverse talent is important when assembling collaborators.

10   According to PC World in an article published on 11 August 2006.

¹¹ *The first four retailers to sell Apple products were Paul Terrell's Byte Shop (Palo Alto, California) plus Itty Bitty Machine Company (Evanston, Illinois), Data Domain (Bloomington, Indiana) and Computer Mart (New York City).*

¹² *As a side note, that first plan included a strategy to establish dedicated Apple stores, a hugely successful concept that took another 25 years to come to fruition.*

¹³ *Collaborative communities must be able to evolve, with the potential for new collaborators to be added while others fall by the wayside. The environment must be flexible enough to support such evolution.*

¹⁴ *Most English speakers actually recognise 15,000-20,000 word families, also known as lemmas, which means that they really know more than this, but since a word lemma is effectively a variation on a theme (like red, reddish, reddest, reddening etc.) it's generally accepted that 15,000-20,000 is a typical native language total word knowledge.*

¹⁵ *The US's second satellite, Vanguard 1, was launched into space on 17 March 1958 and is still in orbit today. It is the world's oldest satellite and unless forcibly removed, it is expected to remain in orbit for another 180 years.*

¹⁶ *Email and digital file transfer didn't appear until the 1970s, although NASA were immediate adopters once those technologies became available.*

¹⁷ *As an aside, a 2013 NASA budget reference document contained 22 pages defining more than 800 acronyms.*

¹⁸ *NASA now specifies 15 decimal places for pi. This is based on the premise that the most distant spacecraft from Earth (Voyager) is 12.5 bn miles away. Using pi rounded to the 15th decimal place we can plot its position accurately to within 4 cm in three-dimensional space—that is generally considered to be 'good enough'.*

¹⁹ *Working to eight significant digits of pi was relatively simple with calculations processed by the IBM 1620 mainframe computer which was available from 1961. For more general calculations, five significant digits were used—a level of detail possible with log tables—and this was accurate to tolerances of 1,000 m – good enough for lunar orbit insertion.*

²⁰ *Before doing an evaluation, it can be a useful exercise to identify approaches that are independent, those that are complementary, and those that are contradictory. Go through each approach (the first level of the ATA framework) and classify each within one of these three categories.*

21 *A common trap when people don't do a risk/reward assessment is to assume that high-risk approaches automatically correlate to high rewards ... but this is not always the case. In fact, it's often not the case. There are often lots of high-risk activities where the reward is minimal.*

22 *But, low-risk/high-reward opportunities typically have a lower probability of success. For example, doing the lottery: excellent reward for minimal risk, but the chances of reward are very slim. So, the probability of success also needs to be considered.*

23 *It's a good idea to break down high-risk approaches into a series of phases. Upon completion of each phase, the approach can be re-assessed and a go/no go decision made before proceeding to the next.*

24 *An increasingly popular activity associated with large endeavour is to conduct a pre-mortem, where a group of collaborators consider everything that could go catastrophically wrong. The risk assessment associated with the definition and sequencing process can directly feed these discussions and focuses attention on the most potentially serious issues, and how their probability of occurrence can be minimised.*

25 *Controlling mechanisms are the tools and processes necessary to manage a project such as: project management software, performance metrics, progress reports, change control procedures, risk management and escalation procedures, quality assurance and control, resource management, communications protocols and project reviews and audits.*

26 *The Moon rotates on its axis every ~27 days. Daytime on one side of the Moon lasts about 13.5 Earth days followed by a night that lasts 13.5 Earth days. In the sunshine, the Moon's surface reaches 127 C (260 F) and in the dark, -173 C (-280 F). At the time of the Apollo missions, the Moon's surface was assumed to be a vacuum but we now know that it actually has an atmosphere amounting to around $3 \times 10 - 15$ atm (0.3 nPa), varying throughout the day, and a total mass of less than 10 metric tonnes. It is primarily composed of (in order of abundance): argon, helium, neon, sodium, potassium and hydrogen.*

27 *NASA engineers O'Kane and Jones designed a space suit helmet and many of their design features became part of the final version.*

28 *This is a useful, but incorrect paraphrase of a quotation attributed to William Deming. The full quote has almost exactly the opposite meaning and says "It is wrong to suppose that if you can't measure it, you can't manage it – a costly myth".*

29 *Monitoring is essential because you get what you inspect rather than what you expect.*

30   *Evaluation also allows for the identification of inefficiencies and bottlenecks, prompting people to proactively address issues and refine processes to enhance overall endeavour performance. It drives transparency, efficiency and, ultimately, success.*

31   *Each KPI should be considered from a leading or lagging perspective. Lagging would be the absolute values. Leading would be the trend line and estimates for future performance. Coincident values would be if a particular KPI is indicative of performance in other areas.*

32   *This is why it's a good idea to have pre-established backup plans. Developing and implementing contingency plans 'on the fly' is challenging.*

33   *This is effectively what happened during the financial crisis of 2008. Individual mortgages were packaged into 'mortgage backed securities' (MBS's) that on the surface looked like a solid investment. As people began to default on their mortgages, it didn't become clear until the point that the MBS's collapsed, quickly followed by the global financial markets.*

34   *Mortgage defaults finally peaked at 11.48% in the first quarter of 2010.*

35   *Looks at the metaphysics of the endeavour. Measured by assessing the general attitude of participants and their motivation to continue. Linked to 'emergence', where the sum of the whole is greater than the parts (or, at the very least, different to the parts).*

36   *In some instances, participants may be going above and beyond assigned responsibilities, indicating extreme engagement.*

37   *As much as possible, evaluation should be undertaken by the individual participants within a collaborative endeavour—those that have responsibility for approaches, tasks and activities. Measurement should be done as close as possible to where the actual work is being undertaken.*

38   *Change Control Boards and Configuration Control Boards were common within Apollo. Change Control Boards were focused on project-level changes such as project documentation and large-scale specifications, including changes to project plans such as adjustments to the project's scope, budget or schedule. Configuration Control Boards were formed to approve and track changes to a product's deliverables and processes and involved a series of reviews and approvals by supervisors, stakeholders and technical experts. Configuration control reduced the risk of failure or malfunction by ensuring that any changes were fully tested before being added to the final product.*

39   *Participants push boundaries for different reasons. Sometimes, it is out of a desire to succeed and they are genuinely striving for the best for the group. Occasionally, it is because of cultural or personality differences. No matter what the reason, conflicts based on people overstepping boundaries need to be carefully monitored and measured.*

40   *Two key dangers of not keeping people informed. First, is that people simply feel left out and disengaged which demotivates. Second, is that people make assumptions about status or succumb to rumour and gossip.*

41   *This is especially important if the endeavour requires effort that is generally considered to be 'above and beyond' normal behaviour.*

42   *"Anything that can go wrong, will." Captain Edward A. Murphy Jr, USAF*

43   *Typically, these will be temporary assignments of short duration, but they can also lead to more permanent positions down the road.*

44   *Demotivators should be either eliminated or isolated, while motivators should be elevated and promoted.*

45   *The* Maiden *crew was: Tracy Edwards (skipper), Mandi Swan (Amanda Swan Neal), Mikaela Von Koskull, Claire Warren, Michele Paret, Tanja Visser, Sally Creaser (not leg 3), Dawn Riley, Nancy Hill, Jeni Mundy, Jo Gooding (from Leg 2), Sarah Davies (leg 3), Kristin Harris (Leg 1) and Angela Farrell.*

46   *Mediate is the opposite of immediate and its root is mediare (to be in the middle), from Latin medius (middle) and originally from the Indo-European root medhyo- (middle), which also spawns middle, mean, medium, medal (originally a coin worth a halfpenny), mezzanine, mediocre, mediterranean, moiety, and mullion.*

47   *Negotiation is when an individual has a direct stake in the outcome. Mediation is when an individual is an impartial third-party or has an indirect stake in a larger outcome.*

48   *Mediation should result in an agreement that is acceptable to all parties. If any one party feels that they were misled, the outcome will not have long-term viability.*

49   *If any party feels that their position—or they themselves—are not respected, the inevitable result is a breakdown of the mediation and a subsequent failure to reach resolution.*

50   *Sometimes, when conflicts are broken down into facts, they are automatically resolved because the reasoning behind the conflict was a lack of clarity.*

51 *It's important to acknowledge the implications of the conflict, since small impacts can rapidly expand into larger existential threats to collaborative endeavours.*

52 *It's useful to conclude with a plan of action/agreement and ensure commitment to it. Establish a monitoring plan with associated checkpoints to ensure that the outcome has been reached and is operating successfully.*

53 *There are lots of examples of advanced research innovation programmes that delivered astonishing fundamental innovations such as the Lockheed Martin 'Skunkworks', Xerox Parc, Google X, and (of course) NASA. But, they had/have massive budgets and substantial staff numbers.*

54 *An interesting study by Nathanael Fast, Chip Heath and George Wu in Psychological Science titled "Common Ground and Cultural Prominence: How Conversation Reinforces Culture", found that people generally prefer to talk about things that are 'easy' to discuss and in which they have some level of knowledge. People tend to find common ground in conversation, focusing on ideas and concepts that are most familiar. That is comfortable, but it suppresses collaborative culture and stifles innovative thinking.*

55 *There are four key types of waves: spilling, plunging, collapsing and surging. Oh, and I suppose tsunamis make five!*

56 *In 1962 IBM employed 130,000 people and brought in revenues of $2.5 bn.*

57 *The Systems Engineer Development (SED) program became a mainstay of EDS culture for forty-five years, right up until EDS was bought by HP in 2008. In 1989, Roger Alderson became a proud graduate of the program.*

58 *Although this business model is known as 'outsourcing' today, in 1969 it was referred to as 'facilities management'.*

59 *Although the concept of continual improvement has been around forever, it was popularised by Masaaki Imai, a Japanese business process theorist, in his 1986 book, "Kaizen, The Key to Japan's Competitive Success".*

60 *Ironically, the more challenging the collaborative endeavour, and the steps to achieve the purpose, the more likely it is that new ideas will be generated from within the participant community.*

61 *A good way to structure 'Future Horizons' discussions is to ask people to consider four categories in which change will happen—governmental, economic, technological and sociological.*

⁶² *A midpoint between Breakthrough Concept and Applied Innovation sessions is to look for adjacent innovation—ideas that are close to or alongside existing approaches.*

⁶³ *The Inca performed multiple cycles of exposing potatoes to below-freezing temperatures on mountain peaks in the Andes during the evening, and squeezing water out and drying them in the sunlight during the day. The Inca people also used the unique climate of the Altiplano to freeze dry meat.*

⁶⁴ *In 1975, Moore updated his prediction to a doubling of IC components every two years, and "Moores Law" still holds true today.*

⁶⁵ *It's worth noting that all endeavours need a principal orchestrator with overall responsibility for achieving the purpose and delivering a successful outcome. But, more complex endeavours can also take advantage of the concept of distributed leadership. This means recognising that some participants will be open to accepting responsibilities beyond their immediate sphere of influence and operating for the broader good of the community. Tapping into this willingness, and delegating some responsibility to these people, can significantly increase an endeavour's potential for success.*

Printed in Great Britain
by Amazon